How to Study The Bible

(The Essentials of Biblical Hermeneutics)

by
Elder Conrad Jarrell

ISBN 978-1-329-88117-4

© Copyright 2010, 2015 by Conrad Owen Jarrell II.

Acknowledgements

I have nothing save what I have been given, so am greatly indebted to others. They being dead yet speak into the ears of my mind and memory (Heb 11:4), and guide me through the years of my sojourn. I give to them only my undying gratitude, for I have no sufficient coin.

To my God and my King, The Lord Jesus Christ.

He gave me Forgiveness and Life and Hope and Faith, and opened my atheist eyes that I might behold wondrous things out of His Law, and with kind Providence led me to three others.

To Elder K. W. Yeager, M.Ed.,
Baptist pastor and retired school teacher in Huntsville, Alabama.

He taught me that before I tell others what The Bible *means*, to first make sure I know precisely what It *says*, for It *means* what It *says*. He grounded me on the supreme importance of the Words of Scripture, and hence the grammar and syntax of Bible passages—for they are Words that were spoken by God Almighty, to men who merely wrote them down, to be frozen in time but thawed in the heart by the Holy Spirit; and that God "did let *none* of His Words fall to the ground." (1 Sam 3:19) He taught me the proper use of interlinear Bible texts, of Hebrew and Greek lexicons, dictionaries and encyclopedias and reference books of all kinds. He put tools in my hands, and taught me to use them, with which I might build the knowledge of a lifetime. He was truly my Father in the ministry (1 Cor 4:15).

To Elder C. E. Smith, Th. D.,
Baptist pastor and retired seminary professor in Shawnee, Oklahoma.

He had *memorized* the entire King James Bible in English, the Greek New Testament, and most of the Hebrew Old Testament. More than once I heard him say, "I used to call myself Dr. C. E. Smith, Th. D.; until God showed me I was only Charlie Smith the Sinner, saved by grace." He taught me the necessity of Study; at times, grinding, relentless study. "Even in a gold mine," he told me, "They have to mine a ton or more of rock to fetch a single ounce of gold. Any fool can pick the rock, but only a workman finds the gold." He taught me the amazing truth that The Bible is It's own best interpreter. One verse is the key to another verse's padlock, Scripture with Scripture (1 Cor 2:13). He taught me that the Hebrew Old Testament was the unmovable bedrock, that the Greek New Testament was the rich top soil, and that the King James English was the crop, bountiful to harvest. "*Never* attempt to correct the English with the Greek and Hebrew." He taught me to observe how the English flourished from nutrients in the Greek and sent its roots deep to mine the minerals of the Hebrew. He grounded me in the absolute and essential uniqueness of the Masoretic Hebrew, the Textus Receptus Greek, and the King James Version English. He showed me how to harvest the grain, grind the flour, and bake the bread, that I and others might eat and prosper. He was my Mentor.

To Elder Norman Cooper,
Baptist pastor in Texas, and retired tradesman and chef, who never graduated from high school.

He taught me the most valuable lessons I have learned about Apologetics and Homiletics. He could swing the Sword of Truth two-handed in battle like God's own Viking. This untaught peasant's son, a true autodidact, would prevail in brutal debate against giants of Academe; and when the battle was done, stand bloodied and black-eyed, and grinning, with his foot on the fallen enemy. He taught me the neatest tricks of how to cut through the conundrums of the scholars, like Alexander cutting the Gordian Knot. Yet I have heard him patiently counseling and teaching a room of college educated adults, who were taking notes. I have seen him walking and joking with teenagers, who hung on his every word. I have watched him sit and play dollies with little girls, and soldiers with little boys, and with a smile and a wink give them quarters, which they treasured. He taught me that the purpose of Battle was not Fame nor Glory, but the defense of God's Children, especially the widows and the fatherless. He taught me to love the wise and the foolish, to nurture the rich and the poor, for they all have their special needs and cry alone in the night. Once, decades ago, when I was young and he was old, I told him I had no way to pay him the debt I owed for his teaching. He replied, "One day, sooner than you think, you will be old and I will be gone. And some young person will sit at your feet and ask, Brother Jarrell, teach me The Word of God. When that happens, just pass it on." Ohhh, God!...sure enough...and sooner than I ever thought. Coop was my Friend.

And so, Kind Reader,
I render into your hands this **token** *payment.*

Contents

Chapter 1—What is The Bible? … 1
- Introduction … 2
- Inspiration of The Bible … 7
- Preservation of The Bible … 18

Chapter 2—Basics of Bible Interpretation … 26
- Introduction … 27
- The 4 Principles of Bible Study … 28
- The 5 Rules of Bible Study … 42

Chapter 3—Getting Down and Dirty (Examples) … 61
- Introduction—7 Core Doctrines … 62
- The Identity of God … 62
- Eternal Election … 65
- Faith OF God vs. Faith IN God … 71
- Regeneration before Faith … 83
- TULIP—The Plan of Salvation … 88
- Tent of Abraham, Tabernacle of Moses, Church of Christ … 97
- Amillennialism vs. *all* other -isms … 106

Chapter 4—Bible Study & Reading (Tools and Tips) … 114
- First Things First … 115
- Good Tools for Bible Study … 115
- Interregnum: How to de-Babel Bible Word Definitions … 120
- Bible Reading Tips … 121

Chapter 5—Some Final Thoughts … 131

Chapter 1—What is The Bible?

Introduction
Inspiration of The Bible
Preservation of The Bible

Introduction

In 2010, when I began this book, in the form of a pamphlet, the first paragraph read like this,

> For many years, I have thought about writing a book on Biblical Hermeneutics. Instead, it turns out to be a booklet of outlines on How to Study The Bible. I suppose that shows what I know. But sometimes, less is better.

Now (2015), I'm going to *start* the whole book with *this* paragraph:

I have decided...finally...to write a *book* on How to Study The Bible, emphasizing what I believe to be *the most basic essentials* of Biblical Hermeneutics. I suppose this stumbling start shows what I know. But sometimes, less is better, to start with.

To begin, let us answer the question, "What is The Bible?" Since this is not a book on manuscript evidence, but guidelines for studying The Bible, I'll just lay out the basic information, then afterwards we'll get on with it.

The Holy Scriptures *Fully* Defined

The Holy Scriptures will be the final authority in this discussion. But, *exactly what* are The Holy Scriptures? For the sake of brevity, we will define them and move on (Manuscript Evidence is a whole 'nother ballgame). The Holy Scriptures in English are those books comprising The Authorized Version of 1611 (AV 1611, King James Version, or KJV), *minus* the Apocrypha. The King James Version was translated *exclusively* from the following Hebrew and Greek Scriptures (the Apocrypha was included in a middle section, the Translators stating they did not believe it to be Scripture, later it was left out entirely). The Holy Scriptures in Hebrew are that collection of books underlying the KJV Old Testament; specifically that used by the Translators, the Daniel Bomberg Edition of 1525, edited by Jacob ben Chayim, and commonly called the Masoretic Text. The Holy Scriptures in Greek are that collection of books underlying the KJV New Testament. The Translators never saw fit to select, or reconstruct, a Greek text, relying primarily upon the *Textus Receptus* editions of Robert Stephens 1550 and 1551, and Beza 1598, but altering them in about 190 places as they felt compelled by the evidence. Cambridge University commissioned F.H.A. Scrivener to produce The Greek Text Underlying the Authorized Version of 1611, and it was published in 1881 (most scholars still consider that edition more reliable than those following). The 1881 Edition of Scrivener's is considered to be The Holy Scriptures in Greek.

Kurt Aland (no friend of the *Textus Receptus*), in his Summary of Manuscript Evidence (1967), tabulates the variant readings (table shown at the end of this section) between the *Textus Receptus* and what we may call the Wescott and Hort Text (based primarily upon Aleph, B, Alexandrinus, and Sinaiticus, all Roman Catholic manuscripts preferred by the new-bible scholars). He used all available sources from the papyri, the uncials, the cursives, and the lectionaries (some 5262 at the time, about 5300 now). Aland estimated that the *Textus Receptus* readings (King James type) dominated the evidence *over 99% of the time,* while the Westcott and Hort readings (the ones preferred by the Roman Catholics and the modern scholars behind the new 'bibles') were found *in less than 1%!* In the lectionaries, those collections of readings copied out by *local churches* for devotional use (and numbering 2143, or 41% of the evidence), *not one single Westcott and Hort (Roman Catholic) reading is found*—the entire pile is composed *solely* of KJV type readings! For anyone even pretending to believe that God both gave and preserved an inspired and infallible Bible, this should be mind-boggling.

The evidence for the Masoretic Text underlying the King James Old Testament is equally compelling. Malachi wrote the last book of the OT about 430 BC. Until the discovery of the Dead Sea Scrolls, the oldest copy of the Masoretic Text was the Aleppo Codex, dated to about 950 AD. Over 1400 years separated the two, and many doubted that Scripture could be copied accurately over such an expanse of time. When the Dead Sea Scrolls were discovered (in the 1940s), and finally collated, identified, and translated, it was found that about 80% of the Biblical scrolls were clearly Masoretic type texts. Furthermore, several careful datings have confirmed that the Biblical Scrolls were written over a period from at least 50 BC to as early as 250 BC. Here's the punch line—The Dead Sea Masoretic Texts and the Middle Ages Masoretic Texts *are virtually identical!* Are there discrepancies? Yes, but except for mostly word order and spelling, and slight differences in marginal notes, the Biblical Text in both is unmistakably the same; and both differ greatly from any other Hebrew textual tradition (Dr. Randall Price, **Secrets of the Dead Sea Scrolls**, 1996, Ch. 6). The Masoretic Text, in the dedicated hands of certain Hebrew scholars, remained *virtually unchanged* for over 1000 years, from 50 BC to 950 BC. This is the text underlying the KJV OT. Again, mind-boggling.

Until some Biblical textual lineage, with manuscript evidence superior to that underlying the King James Bible is brought forth—*and not one has been since 1611*—I affirm that the Authorized Version of

1611 is God's inspired, infallible, and preserved Word in English, and is to be confirmed and validated in *all* textual questions by reference *only* to the underlying Hebrew Masoretic Text and Greek *Textus Receptus*, as both are defined above.

For the rest...

As I said above, sometimes less is better. I have decided to be concise rather than exhaustive. Rather than tell you every useful thing I ever read or heard about Bible Study, I have determined to show you those few *essential* things, without which none of the rest really matters. You can buy a book or two on hermeneutics, or borrow and read many of them for yourself. I am just going to show you the *essentials*. If you have these essentials, yet never get around to reading another book on Bible study, you will do alright. If you read every book in the world, get yourself a Ph.D., and teach Hermeneutics in a seminary, yet *do not have these essentials* down pat, you will be as useless as a chicken squawking in a windstorm.

Hermeneutics is a fifty-cent word that was adopted c. 1737 into English from the Greek word *hermeneuo*, which means "to interpret." The dictionary tells us that *interpret* means "to explain the meaning or significance of something." Thus, Biblical Hermeneutics endeavors to explain the meaning of passages of Scripture. But, what if You are reading The Bible *alone*? What if there is no 'Splainifier' handy? How do *You* crack those tough nut passages? In other words, how do You, reading alone, *perceive* the meaning of Bible passages?

When I use the term Biblical Hermeneutics in this book, I mean two things. **FIRSTLY**, Biblical Hermeneutics as I am going to teach it, means that collection of concepts, principles, and rules which will enable You, Child of God, while reading alone, to perceive with confidence what The Bible that your Father sent you *means*. I intend to teach You that The Bible *means* exactly what It *says*—and how You can *know* it...beyond *reasonable* doubt.

Unfortunately, if you are not a Child of God, what I have to say will seem only drivel. Even to a lost seminary professor who teaches Hermeneutics, it will seem foolish, because it isn't what he teaches. God wrote The Bible only to His Children, and only they can understand and treasure it.

> Matt 4:10-12 And **when he was alone, they that were about him with the twelve** asked of him the parable.
> 11 And he said unto them, **Unto you it is given to know the mystery of the kingdom of God: but unto them that are without, all *these* things are done in parables:** 12 That seeing they may see, and not perceive; and hearing

they may hear, and not understand; lest at any time they should be converted, and *their* sins should be forgiven them.
 13 And he said unto them, Know ye not this parable? and how then will ye know all parables?

How then will *You* know all parables? If you are a Child of God, I will show you. And how can you know that you are a Child of God? Pay close attention, not to me, but to the Words of God that I cite. When I have told you the best I can, then look closely at them. Ask yourself, Is that what they *say*? Is that what they *mean*? You might have to pray to God about it, like the disciples above asked Jesus. But, you may feel like, I don't know how to pray, I don't know how to talk to God about such. Don't worry about that. Just fumble ahead, God knows what you are trying to say; He knows what you need before you know how to ask (please read Isa 65:24). There is nothing mystical about this, nothing at all. When I show you what a Bible verse *says*, and then tell you what it *means*, just ask yourself (and ask God, for a double check)—*Are they both the same?* If they are, that's how you know all parables; because, things that are the same are not different. It works like this,

> Jer 6:16-17 Thus saith the LORD, Stand ye in the ways, and see, and ask for the old paths, where *is* the good way, and walk therein, and ye shall find rest for your souls. But they said, We will not walk *therein*. 17 Also I set watchmen over you, *saying*, Hearken to the sound of the trumpet. But they said, We will not hearken.

Some will not see. Some cannot hear. From the Gate of the Garden of Eden to the Battle of Armageddon, there is only one group of people who ever do See the Way and Hear the Trumpet. So, watch carefully, listen closely. I'll show you, best I can.

Bible Hermeneutics is simply How to Study The Bible...how *You*, all alone, can study The Bible, with confidence of understanding. It is just that simple. Literally, even a child can do it.

> Act 17:11-12a These were more noble than those in Thessalonica, in that **they received the word** with all readiness of mind, **and searched the scriptures** daily, whether those things were so. 12 **Therefore many of them believed**...

> 2 Tim 3:15 And that **from a child thou hast known the holy scriptures,** which are able to make thee wise unto salvation through faith which is in Christ Jesus.

SECONDLY, when I use the term Biblical Hermeneutics, I mean *emphatically* that collection of concepts, principles, and rules of Bible Study *that The Bible explicitly states as such.* No, there is no chapter in The Bible entitled How to Study The Bible. But, every one of the concepts, principles, and rules of Bible Study that I will teach you *are* stated explicitly in The Bible—*I will cite them plainly, and they will read so plainly.* For years, I have had people say about the things I'm going to show you, "Aww, Conrad Jarrell just made that stuff up." I cannot tell you how many times I have *read a Bible verse* to someone in the course of a discussion, and that person has responded, "That's just your opinion." No, if I *read* a Bible verse that *says* it, *it's God's opinion.* Which brings up a pertinent point. My job as a preacher is not to convert people. No, it really isn't. My job is not to recruit people into churches. My job is not to change people. *My job is to TELL people.* That is also the job of every Believer in this world, no exceptions. Just *tell* people. *Just tell people.* God will do the changing, and the converting, and the drawing. Preachers and Believers JUST TELL PEOPLE.

> Isa 43:10-12 **Ye *are* my witnesses, saith the LORD**, and my servant whom I have chosen: that ye may know and believe me, and understand that I *am* he: before me there was no God formed, neither shall there be after me. 11 I, *even* I, *am* the LORD; and beside me *there is* no saviour. 12 I have declared, and have saved, and I have showed, when *there was* no strange *god* among you: **therefore ye *are* my witnesses, saith the LORD, that I *am* God.**

> Jn 7:14-18 **I have given them thy word**; and the world hath hated them, because they are not of the world, even as I am not of the world. 15 I pray not that thou shouldest take them out of the world, but that thou shouldest keep them from the evil. 16 They are not of the world, even as I am not of the world. 17 Sanctify them through thy truth: thy word is truth. 18 **As thou hast sent me into the world, even so have I also sent them into the world**.

> 1 Jn 5:10-13 **He that believeth on the Son of God hath the witness in himself:** he that believeth not God hath made him a liar; because he believeth not the record that God gave of his Son. 11 **And this is the record, that God hath given to us eternal life, and this life is in his Son.** 12 He that hath the Son hath life; *and* he that hath not the Son of God hath not life. 13 **These things have I written unto you that believe on the name of the Son of God; that ye may know that ye have eternal life, and that ye may believe on the name of the Son of God.**

Jn 6:44-45 **No man can come to me, except the Father which hath sent me draw him**: and I will raise him up at the last day. 45 It is written in the prophets, And they shall be all taught of God. **Every man therefore that hath heard, and hath learned of the Father, cometh unto me.**

So as the saying goes, when I have told people, *Then they done been told*. Watch carefully, listen closely. I'll tell you, best I can.

The Inspiration of The Bible

The A.V. 1611 is the *only* Word of God in English. You see, all the modern versions of the Bible...*without exception*...are based upon the textual theories of Westcott & Hort, the men most responsible for the English Revised Version of 1881. They sought to replace the textual tradition of the King James Bible with that of Roman Catholic manuscripts (primarily Aleph, B, Alexandrinus, and Sinaiticus), differing in thousands of places, from not only the King James text, *but from each other*. Knowing this, consider what these two men *admitted in print* about their motives and methods in producing this new version:

Westcott, on the Changes in Readings:

> "The value of the Revision is most clearly seen when the student considers together a **considerable** group of passages, which bear upon some article of faith. **The accumulation of small details then produces its full effect.**" (Streeter, **The Four gospels**, 1930, p. 30)

Hort, on the Changes in Readings:

> "I do not think the significance of their [the changes, COJ] existence is generally understood. It is quite impossible to judge the value of **what appears to be trifling alterations** merely by reading them one after another. **Taken together, they have often important bearings which few would think of at first.**" (**Life of Hort**, vol. 2, p. 102)

Hort, on the New Revision (RSV, 1881) that they were planning (emphases mine, COJ):

> "The errors and prejudices, which we agree in wishing to remove, can surely be more wholesomely and also **more effectively reached by individual efforts of an indirect kind** than by combined open assault. At present very many orthodox but rational men are being **unawares acted on by influences which will assuredly bear good fruit in due time, if the process is al-**

lowed to go on quietly; but I cannot help fearing that a premature crisis would frighten back many into the merest traditionalism." (Hort, **Life & Letters**, vol. 1, p. 400; to Rowand Williams, 21 Oct 1858, 23 years *before* the new Revision!)

I think it impossible for any rational person, given those above quotes, to defend as honest the Westcott and Hort Tradition, which lies behind *all* the new modern revised versions. In the face of the evidence, such a defense would amount to *ethical* criminality. Police use three quick tests to determine Criminal Intent: Motive, Method, and Opportunity.

What was the MOTIVE of Westcott & Hort (and all their new-bible copycats)? To *change* the readings of Holy Scripture, attested by the evidence of ages, into *Something Different*. Can we prove that? Sure —*Read their own words quoted above.*

What was the METHOD that Westcott & Hort (and all their new-bible copycats) used to make their work seem *Credible*? To finagle, dissemble, and inveigle *different* preferred readings from Roman Catholic texts into something *proffered* as God's Word. Can we prove that? Sure—*Read their own words quoted above.*

Did Westcott & Hort (and all their new-bible copycats) have genuine and specific OPPORTUNITY to commit such a dastardly prevarication? Manifestly...consider quote 3—where it is revealed they planned it *for over 23 years, fearful they might be exposed*—until they published their fraudulent 'bible' in 1881. Can we prove that? Sure— *Read their own words quoted above*, then remember that *they did exactly that in 1881*; then remember that all their new-bible copycats have done *exactly that* with every single new revised bible, *without a single exception.*

Motive, Method, Opportunity—all the basic legal proof required to show Criminal Intent. I ASSEVERATE (look it up) that *ALL* new revised 'bibles' since the A.V. 1611, following the Roman Catholic manuscript *modus operandi* of Westcott & Hort and their new-bible copycats, are fallacious and fraudulent, and thus are evidence of *ethical* criminality. Can I prove that? I just did. Furthermore, over 50 years of preaching the Word of God and Defending the Faith against Gainsayers have convinced me: That *explicit* Asseveration is beyond *successful* Contestation.

So, I say again: The A.V. 1611 is the *only* Word of God in English. When learning How to Study The Bible, anything and everything... *Different*...proffered as 'a bible,' may confidently be tossed aside as Demonic Deception and Drivel. Proof? You mean, even *more*? Try this:

> 1 Tim 4:1-2 Now the Spirit speaketh **expressly**, that **in the latter times** some shall depart from the faith, giving heed to **seducing spirits, and doctrines of devils**; 2 **Speaking lies in hypocrisy**; having their conscience seared with a hot iron;

From 1611 forward, *all* times are more latter than *any* times previous, back to Creation. And 1611 time is at least 1,544 years more latter than 61-67 AD, when Paul wrote 1 Timothy. Moving on from that basis, let us once more *define* Holy Scripture.

The Holy Scriptures *Concisely* Defined

Subsuming the evidence offered above (see The Holy Scriptures *More Fully* Defined, pp. 2-3), here is a *concise* definition of The Holy Scriptures.

The Holy Scriptures in **English**—those books comprising The Authorized Version of 1611 (AV 1611, King James Version, or KJV), *minus* the Apocrypha.

The Holy Scriptures in **Hebrew**—that collection of books underlying the KJV Old Testament; specifically that used by the Translators, the Daniel Bomberg Edition of 1525, edited by Jacob ben Chayim, and commonly called the Masoretic Text.

The Holy Scriptures in **Greek**—that collection of books underlying the KJV New Testament. Cambridge University commissioned F.H.A. Scrivener to produce The Greek Text Underlying the Authorized Version of 1611, and it was published in 1881 (most scholars still consider that edition more reliable than those following). The 1881 Edition of Scrivener's is considered to be The Holy Scriptures in Greek.

That is The Bible I will try my best to teach you How to Study.

Two Kinds of Inspiration

Since the word "inspiration" only appears in two passages in the entire Bible, let's just quote 'em all...and add just one extra, which is going to prove exquisitely helpful.

> Job 32:8 But there is a spirit in man: and the **inspiration** of the Almighty giveth them **understanding**.

> 2 Tim 3:16-17 **All <u>scripture</u> is given by <u>inspiration</u> of God**, and is **profitable** <u>for doctrine, for reproof, for correction, for instruction in righteousness</u>: 17 That the man of God may be **perfect**, <u>thoroughly furnished unto all good works</u>.

1 Sam 3:19 And Samuel grew, and the LORD was with him, and did let none of his words fall to the ground.

Pay special attention to that last verse. If you graduated from a government high school any time after about 1965, you are going to need a brain crutch to hobble through it.

BRAIN CRUTCH. In order to dumb-down voters, so they would be stupid enough to vote in Socialism (which they finally did in 2012)—which means legally stealing money from those who earned it, then giving it to bums who didn't, to buy their votes (as Karl Marx recommended)—the government schools, in the mid to late 60s, severely crippled the teaching of Grammar. They did so by ripping out the teaching and defining of THE 8 PARTS OF SPEECH (Gee! You don't know what those are? Imagine that!). Then, they uprooted and cast out the Introductory Basics of Logic, by tossing out DIAGRAMMING SENTENCES, which means drawing a simple diagram of a sentence, showing how the Parts of Speech that compose it precisely fit together, so you can *see* exactly what it *says*, and therefore *know* exactly what it *means*. What? You don't have a clue what I'm talking about? I bet you graduated from high school after 1965. How did I know that? Lucky guess. I was taught basic grammar and the parts of speech in primary grades. I was taught advanced grammar and diagramming sentences in middle school. I was taught advanced grammar and basic logic in high school. All in government schools...*way back Then* (I'm 74 now, in 2015). If you are younger than about 65 years old, went to government schools, and *don't know this stuff* (even if you have a Ph.D. from Harvard)...then, you done been screwed. Your brain has been busted at the knees, and you have to crawl through muddy words like a slug. To stand up out of the sludge and hobble, you are going to need a Brain Crutch. The handle allowing a sure grip is THE 8 PARTS OF SPEECH. The staff, securely attached to the handle, for steady movement (through word sludge) is DIAGRAMMING SENTENCES. With this Brain Crutch firmly in your grasp, you will be capable of Basic Logic, without even realizing it. Without a Brain Crutch? Well...look down at that there slug...(even if you have a Ph.D. from Harvard). I mean, *Look how many times you had to go back and re-read this paragraph!* See?

HOW TO GET A BRAIN CRUTCH. The first thing you need is *assurance* that government has indeed played these head games I have described. I recommend the little book **The War Against Grammar**, by David Mulroy, 2003. Think of it as the instruction sheet about how to grip the handle then swing the crutch, in simple diagram form. Then, to actually take the parts out of the cellophane and assemble them all together, the best single book I have ever found is **English Composition,** by Charles H. Vivian and Bernetta M. Jackson, 1961 (my dogeared edition), Barnes & Noble College Outline Series #102. Basic Grammar, Sentence Diagramming, Basic Composition, Clear Thinking and Introductory Logic—Everything you need for picking up sludgy words, cleaning them up, putting them properly into correct sentences, paragraphs, and even reports and books (gasp!), along with basic logic and reasoning guidelines. Most people will be able to do fine with this one book. Sadly, after being in print for decades, it seems to have lapsed. Used copies are available at Amazon and AbeBooks.com. But, whatever you settle for, it *must* have, at the very least, THE 8 PARTS OF SPEECH (or Basic Grammar) and SENTENCE DIAGRAMMING.

Wanna go bear hunting? *Serious* about Grammar and Syntax, and Advanced Logic? Two books...period...no compromise. **The Trivium: The Liberal Arts of Logic, Grammar, and Rhetoric**, by Sister Miriam Joseph and Marguerite McGlinn (2002)—This is your Grammar Book. **Socratic Logic: A Logic Text using Socratic Method, Platonic Questions, and Aristotelian Principles**, Ed. 3.1, by Peter Kreeft and Trent Dougherty (2010)—This is your Logic Book. Yes, they are both Roman Catholic. Yes, the Roman Catholic Manuscripts mentioned above are Satan's Bible for Endtimes. Yes, both these books contain *some* points of Roman Catholic Doctrine. However, Catholics, for some odd reason, are *extremely* careful to make a distinction between Philosophy and Religion...and these are *Philosophy* Books, not *Religion* Books. Both of these authors make that same careful distinction, nor do they try to sneak up and stab you in the back. When they write on Religion, they write *religiously* (Kreeft for instance has written a number of strictly Religious Books); when they write on Philosophy, they write *philosophically*. Just keep your eyes...and your mind...open. But, when taken together, for handling words on paper and ideas in your mind, these two books are a true double-whammy. They contain the *linguistic* best of a classical education—composed of Grammar, Logic, and Rhetoric—dating back over a thousand years, with roots that reach back before the Time of Christ. You can hold 'em in your hand like a baseball bat, walk right up to Noam Chomsky, and knock him staggering (because of his *bad* stuff, not his *good* stuff). You don't know who that is? Then forget it. Stick with **English Composition** by Vivian and Jackson.

Now, let's get back to 1 Sam 3:19b, "the LORD was with him, and did let none of his words fall to the ground." 1 Sam 3:19 is a compound sentence, that means a sentence composed of two or more clauses (little bitty sentences that could stand alone if you didn't jam them together). 1 Sam 3:19b is a compound clause (a little bitty sentence that has two or more main verbs). The Subject of 1 Sam 3:19b, the Noun (a person, place, or thing) that is doing all the action, is "The LORD". The LORD is doing two main actions in the clause, "was" and "did let". Here is The Biggy...*because* it is The LORD that is doing the 'did let'-ing, it is The LORD'S words The LORD did let "none of" fall to the ground—*The LORD did let none of The LORD'S words fall to the ground.* Why is that so important? Follow along with me.

Two kinds of Inspiration

Inscriptive Inspiration (2 Tim 3:16), where God through His Spirit gives words to human authors who write them down (precisely why the words written down are called Scripture).

Understanding Inspiration (Job 32:8), whereby God through His Spirit guides certain of His ministers to recognize infallibly His words of Scripture once written down by Inscriptive Inspiration—so they can accurately *copy* the original text (in *some* textual lines of manuscripts); and so they can *collate and edit* scattered and corrupted manuscripts back into accurate copies of the original text; and so they can accurately *translate* accurate copies of the original text, into another language version, as accurate as the original text.

Here is why 1 Sam 3:19b is such a biggy. It is a proof text for the Doctrine of *Divine Preservation of Scripture.* In every stage of Understanding Inspiration—Copying of Scripture, Collating and Editing Manuscripts containing Scripture, and Translating Scripture into other languages—God through His Spirit so directs the process, that *all the way* from the original autographs none of His words do fall to the ground; thus the final production of *Divinely Preserved* Copied and Translated Scripture (in *some* textual lines of manuscripts) is as authentic, word for word, as the original autographs (because of 1 Sam 3:19b, and of course, other verses).

Two Unbelieving Theories of Inspiration

There are two very popular theories of Inspiration that underly virtually all of the modern revised bible versions. Both of them assume that somehow, as badly as God wanted folks to have a Bible, it kinda sorta got all screwed up through the centuries, and lots of God's Words just fell to the ground. So, these brilliant and educated new modern bible revisers are going to help poor God get His Scripture scotch-taped back together. But, before they can scotch-tape all those words *back* together, they need to know how they all *started out* together...you know, in those original autographs, "long long ago, in a galaxy far far away." So, they've got these here two theories.

One of them is called the NATURAL INSPIRATION THEORY— "Just as some people are gifted with natural ability to paint or compose music, some people are naturally gifted with the ability to make up goddy stories." This theory asks us to believe that a *natural* ability (like somebody juggling 15 raw eggs) is the same as *divine* inspiration (*God* telling *somebody else* to write some words down). I know that's a stretch, but a lot of Ph.D.s in the Harvard Divinity School believe that. So do some of the editors of the modern revised bible versions. IF that *were* true, then some of those modern revised bible versions... *logically*...could be as inspired as some of the original autographs. Makes me wonder, though, *Whom* do they pray to...and *Why* bother? Just saying.

What does The Bible *say*? It *says* that God inspired men to write on specific subjects—the human writers didn't think *anything* up. They were told what to write about, and what to write down in every single sentence, thus every single verse, in The Bible. Not one Bible writer ever thought up even a single sentence just by himself.

> Isa 8:1 Moreover **the LORD <u>said unto</u> me**, **Take thee a great roll, and write in it with a man's pen concerning** Mahershalalhashbaz.

Unless we are willing to *seriously* argue, that *every* Bible writer was insane, with Multiple Personality Disorder, scribbling down lengthy conversations he had with HIMSELVES, that verse pretty well chucks Natural Inspiration Theory. Isn't that weird? Aren't some new revised bible version editors strange?

The other popular theory, embraced by other Ph.D.s in the Harvard Divinity School, along with many other new revised bible version editors, is CONCEPTUAL INSPIRATION, sometimes called Dynamic Inspiration—"God inspired the general ideas, leaving it up to the various writers to word them as they thought best." Kinda like they imagine God just pooted into the writers' heads, and left it up to them to decide whether it stank like beans or bad eggs. Sorry, that's what it smells like to me...both when I first read it in a college textbook, and still today after 50 years of Bible Study. What does The Bible *say* about *how* God inspired the human writers of Scripture? The Bible *says* that the very words, and even the letters of the words were inspired by God (by the way, this is called MECHANICAL DICTATION).

> <u>All of the Words...</u>
>
> Mark 13:31 Heaven and earth shall pass away: but **<u>my</u> <u>words</u>** shall not pass away.
>
> Jer 11:1-3,6 **The <u>word</u> that came to Jeremiah from the LORD, saying, 2 Hear ye the <u>words</u> of this covenant**, and speak unto the men of Judah, and to the inhabitants of Jerusalem; 3 And say thou unto them, Thus saith the LORD God of Israel; **Cursed be the man that obeyeth not the <u>words</u> of this covenant**,...6 Then **the LORD said <u>unto</u> me, Proclaim all these <u>words</u>** in the cities of Judah, and in the

streets of Jerusalem, saying, **Hear ye the <u>words</u> of this covenant, and do <u>them</u>.**

<u>...and even the Letters:</u>

Matt 5:18 For verily **I say <u>unto</u> you**, Till heaven and earth pass,**<u> one jot or one tittle</u> shall in no wise pass from the law, till all be fulfilled**.

Gal 3:16 Now to Abraham and his seed were the promises made. **He saith not, And to <u>seeds, as of many</u>; but <u>as of one, And to thy seed</u>, which is Christ.**

Let's look at a few more brief passages that put all this together, and show us how God uses MECHANICAL DICTATION to *inspire* all the letters and words and sentences of Scripture together, for His chosen ministers to write down, and for His Children to read.

2SA 23:1-2 Now these be the last words of David. David the son of Jesse said, and the man who was raised up on high, the anointed of the God of Jacob, and the sweet psalmist of Israel, said, 2 **The Spirit of the LORD spake by me, and his word was in my tongue.**

PSA 45:1 My heart is inditing a good matter: I speak of the things which I have made touching the king: **my tongue is the pen of a ready writer.**

JER 36:2,4,17-18 Take thee a roll of a book, and **write therein all the words that I have spoken unto thee** against Israel, and against Judah, and against all the nations, from the day I spake unto thee, from the days of Josiah, even unto this day...4 Then Jeremiah called Baruch the son of Neriah: and **Baruch wrote from the mouth of Jeremiah all the words of the LORD, which he had spoken unto him, upon a roll of a book**...17 And they asked Baruch, saying, Tell us now, How didst thou write all these words at his mouth? 18 Then Baruch answered them, **He pronounced all these words unto me with his mouth, and I wrote them with ink in the book.**

NOTE—You have to make it *real plain* for professional scholars!

The Structure of The Bible—It's a Closed Book!

The Bible is *not* an ordinary book. It is *not* just another piece of literature, like Shakespeare, the Bhagavad Gita, a Mickey Mouse comic book, or The Living Bible (TLB is a *paraphrase—neither* a copy *nor* a translation—that means ALL *the words fell to the ground*). Just as God used Inscriptive Inspiration and Understanding Inspiration so that His chosen servants could write, copy, and translate

Scripture; just so, He uses Understanding Inspiration (though in lesser amounts) so that His *obedient* Children can understand it.

First, let's see some Bible verses that teach this is *generally* true:

> ECC 3:11 He hath made every thing beautiful in his time: also **he hath set the world in their heart, so that no man can find out the work that God maketh from the beginning to the end**.

> 1CO 1:18-21 For **the preaching of the cross is to them that perish foolishness; but unto us which are saved it is the power of God.** 19 For it is written, I will destroy the wisdom of the wise, and will bring to nothing the understanding of the prudent. 20 Where is the wise? where is the scribe? where is the disputer of this world? **hath not God made foolish the wisdom of this world?** 21 For after that in the wisdom of God **the world by wisdom knew not God, it pleased God by the foolishness of preaching to save them that believe**.

> LUK 24:32,45 And they said one to another, Did not our heart burn within us, while he talked with us by the way, and while **he opened to us the scriptures**?...45 Then **opened he their understanding, that they might understand the scriptures**,

> ACT 16:14 And a certain woman named **Lydia**, a seller of purple, of the city of Thyatira, which worshipped God, heard us: **whose heart the Lord opened, that she attended unto the things which were spoken of Paul**.

> EPH 1:17 That the God of our Lord Jesus Christ, the Father of glory, may give unto you **the spirit of wisdom and revelation in the knowledge of him**:

See? The Bible is *not* an ordinary book. Next, let's see some Bible verses that show *specifically* that The Bible is a Closed Book, which His Children need His help to understand.

Its doctrine is *Hidden*:

> LUK 8:9-10 And **his disciples** asked him, saying, What might this parable be? 10 And he said, **Unto you it is given to know** the mysteries of the kingdom of God: **but to others in parables**; that seeing they might not see, and hearing they might not understand.

Its doctrine is *Revealed*:

> 1CO 2:9-12 But as it is written, Eye hath not seen, nor ear heard, neither have entered into the heart of man, **the things which God hath prepared for them that love him**. 10 But **God hath revealed them unto us by his Spirit**: for the Spirit searcheth all things, yea, the deep things of God. 11 For what man knoweth the things of a man, save the spirit of man which is in him? even so **the things of God knoweth no man, but the Spirit of God**. 12 Now **we have received**, not the spirit of the world, but **the spirit which is of God; that we might know the things that are freely given to us of God**.

Its doctrine is *Scattered*:

> ISA 28:9-13 **Whom shall he teach** knowledge? and **whom shall he make to understand** doctrine? **them that are weaned from the milk, and drawn from the breasts.** [i.e., His Children, COJ] 10 For precept must be upon precept, precept upon precept; line upon line, line upon line; **here a little, and there a little**: 11 For with stammering lips and another tongue will he speak to this people. 12 To whom he said, This is the rest wherewith ye may cause the weary to rest; and this is the refreshing: yet they would not hear. 13 But the word of the LORD was unto them precept upon precept, precept upon precept; line upon line, line upon line; **here a little, and there a little**; that they might go, and fall backward, and be broken, and snared, and taken.

Its doctrine is *Concentrated*:

> 2TI 2:15 Study to **shew thyself approved unto God**, a workman that needeth not to be ashamed, **rightly dividing the word of truth.**

See? The Bible is *not* an ordinary book.

SUMMARY OF MANUSCRIPT EVIDENCE (Kurt Aland, 1967)

This table summarizes the Manuscript Evidence supporting the *Textus Receptus* Greek New Testament

	Westcott & Hort	Textus Receptus	Total	%WH/TR
Papyri	13	75	88	15%/85%
Uncials	9	258	267	3%/97%
Cursives	23	2741	2764	1%/99%
Lectionaries	0	2143	2143	0%/100%
Totals	45	5217	5262	<u><1%/>99%</u>

GOOD ADVICE

Come to The Bible on your knees.
Confess your ignorance and stupidity to God.
Beg Him to open your heart to understand His Word.

THE BIBLE IS NOT AN ORDINARY BOOK.

The Preservation of The Bible

These five passages of Scripture sum up this topic perfectly:

> NEH 9:5 Then the Levites, Jeshua, and Kadmiel, Bani, Hashabniah, Sherebiah, Hodijah, Shebaniah, and Pethahiah, said, Stand up and bless the LORD your God for ever and ever: and **blessed be thy glorious name, which is exalted above all blessing and praise**.

—Taken together with—

> PSA 138:2 I will worship toward thy holy temple, and praise thy name for thy lovingkindness and for thy truth: for **thou hast magnified thy word above all thy name**.

> Titus 1:1-2 Paul, a servant of God, and an apostle of Jesus Christ, **according to the faith of God's elect, and the acknowledging of the truth which is after godliness**; 2 In hope of eternal life, which **God, that cannot lie**, promised before the world began;

> 1JO 5:9-10 If we receive the witness of men, **the witness of God is greater**: for this is the witness of God which he hath testified of his Son. 10 He that believeth on the Son of God hath the witness in himself: **he that believeth not God hath made him a liar**; because he believeth not the record that God gave of his Son.

> 1SA 3:1,7,19,21 And the child Samuel ministered unto the LORD before Eli. And the word of the LORD was precious in those days; there was no open vision....7 Now Samuel did not yet know the LORD, neither was the word of the LORD yet revealed unto him....19 And Samuel grew, **and the LORD was with him, and did let none of his words fall to the ground**....21 **And the LORD appeared again in Shiloh: for the LORD revealed himself to Samuel in Shiloh by the word of the LORD**.

Observe. God's Name (what the Jews call *HaShem*, The Name) is exalted *above* all blessing and praise...but...The Word of God (what English speaking Christians call The King James Bible, along with the noted Hebrew and Greek texts underlying) *God Himself* has exalted *above* all His Name! Furthermore, if *anybody* rejects The Word of God (The King James Bible as noted, for English speakers), that person *is calling God, Who cannot lie, a liar!* Finally, in *some* lines of manuscripts, from original autographs through multiple copies to translations in other languages (like English), *God has let none of His*

Words fall to the ground. All this so that, in His own good time, God can *reveal* Himself to His Children *by The Word of The LORD*: Whosoever believeth that Jesus is the Christ is born of God (1 John 5:1a).

See? The Bible is *not* an ordinary book. I say again, it is a Book dictated word for word by God Himself, to servants He inspired to write it down, copy it, and even translate it, word for word—without one single word *ever* falling to the ground—both to *reveal* Himself to the Saved and for *public testimony* against the Damned…and on Judgement Day, it will be the single law book in His Hand: In the day when God shall judge the secrets of men by Jesus Christ <u>according to my gospel</u> (Rom 2:16). The Bible is *not* an ordinary book.

Because this concept of the Divine Preservation of *every* word of Scripture is so important, I'm going to nail it to the bedrock with railroad spikes, to provide a solid foundation for How to Study The Bible. First, we'll nail down the Preservation of the Old Testament, and then the Preservation of the New Testament.

The Preservation of the Old Testament

Here are some passages which say that God will preserve His Word. Of course, they apply equally to both Testaments. But, because they are all Old Testament passages, they apply most certainly to the Old Testament.

GOD WILL PRESERVE HIS WORD.

> PSA 119:152,160 Concerning **thy testimonies**, I have known of old that **thou hast founded them for ever.**…160 Thy word is true from the beginning: and **every one of thy righteous judgments endureth for ever.**

> PSA 111:7-8 The works of his hands are verity and judgment; **all his commandments are sure.** 8 **They stand fast for ever and ever,** and are done in truth and uprightness.

> ECC 3:14 I know that, **whatsoever God doeth, it shall be for ever: nothing can be put to it, nor any thing taken from it**: and God doeth it, that men should fear before him.

> ISA 40:8 The grass withereth, the flower fadeth: but **the word of our God shall stand for ever.**

In other words, The Lord did let none of His Words fall to the ground (1Sa 3:19). You see, The Bible is *not* an ordinary book.

3 Problems to Overcome in the Preservation of Scripture:

1. <u>Men LOSE It...God finds It.</u>

> 2KI 22:8 And Hilkiah the high priest said unto Shaphan the scribe, I have found the book of the law in the house of the LORD. And Hilkiah gave the book to Shaphan, and he read it.
>
> —Taken together with—
>
> 2CH 34:14-15 And when they brought out the money that was brought into the house of the LORD, Hilkiah the priest found a book of the law of the LORD **given by Moses**[1]. 15 And Hilkiah answered and said to Shaphan the scribe, I have found the book of the law in the house of the LORD. And Hilkiah delivered the book to Shaphan.
>
>> [1] Heb. *BeYiDH-MSHeh* = Heb., "by the hand of Moses." There are 15 places in the Old Testament which mention "the law of Moses" and "book of Moses," yet this is the only place that says, "by the hand of Moses." Most likely, they found the original autograph in the handwriting of Moses, which had been stored away and forgotten.

2. <u>Men REFUSE It...God confirms it.</u>

> Read EZR 4:1–6:15. The Jews show their adversaries proof from their records (Scripture) that they have permission to rebuild, but the evidence is refused. The adversaries complain to the king, and the Jews tell him where in his records he can find permission for them to rebuild. The king looks...there it is...Scripture vindicated.

3. <u>Men ABUSE It...God restores It.</u>

> JER 36:22–24, 27–28,32 Now the king sat in the winterhouse in the ninth month: and there was a fire on the hearth burning before him. 23 And it came to pass, that **when Jehudi had read three or four leaves, he cut it with the penknife, and cast it into the fire that was on the hearth, until all the roll was consumed in the fire** that was on the hearth. 24 Yet they were not afraid, nor rent their garments, neither the king, nor any of his servants that heard all these words....27 **Then the word of the LORD came to Jeremiah**, after that the king had burned the roll, and the words which Baruch wrote at the mouth of Jeremiah, **saying, 28 Take thee again another roll, and write in it all the former words that were in the first roll**, which Jehoiakim the king of Judah hath burned....32 Then took Jeremiah another roll, and gave it to Baruch the scribe, the son of Neriah; who wrote therein

from the mouth of Jeremiah all the words of the book which Jehoiakim king of Judah had burned in the fire: and **there were added besides unto them many like* words**.

> * Note—Not "many additional words," but "many *like* words;" i.e., variant *synonymous* readings *God Himself inserted into the autographs*—neither *additional* revelation (as the Scofield Bible footnote claims), nor *dichotomous* (different or contrary) variant readings (as Higher Criticism claims)! This is a beautiful example of God taking the wise in their own craftiness (cp. Job 5:13; also 1Cor 3:19-20; Eph 4:14; 2Cor 4:2; cp. Luk 20:23).

JESUS USED A LETTER-PERFECT OLD TESTAMENT

JOH 10:35 If he called them gods [Psa 8:6], unto whom the word of God came, and **the scripture cannot be broken**;

MAT 5:18 For verily I say unto you, **Till heaven and earth pass, one jot[1] or one tittle[2] shall in no wise pass from the law, till all be fulfilled.**

> [1] The *yod* (׳), the smallest Heb. letter.

> [2] Distinguishing marks on similar Heb. letters: ה ת ח ; ד ר.

LUK 16:17 And it is easier for heaven and earth to pass, **than one tittle of the law to fail**.

> Note—The <u>Old Testament Canon</u> (books of the Bible officially recognized as Holy Scripture) is indicated by the following passages:

> LUK 24:44–45 And he said unto them, These are the words which I spake unto you, while I was yet with you, that all things must be fulfilled, which were written in **the law** of Moses, and in **the prophets**, and in **the psalms**, concerning me. 45 Then opened he their understanding, that they might understand **the scriptures**,

>> Observe the 3 Main Divisions of the Hebrew Bible, cited by Josephus, the Jewish historian of the period, and occurring in the Hebrew Masoretic Text. The books he named are the same as found in the Authorized Version of 1611 (KJV) Old Testament.

> MAT 23:35 That upon you may come all the righteous blood shed upon the earth, from the blood of righteous Abel [in the <u>first book</u> of the Hebrew Bible] unto the blood of Zacharias son of Barachias, whom ye slew between the temple and the altar [in the <u>last book</u> of the Hebrew Bible].

Note—The *precise order* of books indicated is that of the Hebrew Masoretic Text, from which the Authorized Version of 1611 (KJV) is translated. Please observe that the Scholars' dearly beloved Septuagint has a different order of books—thus we *know* JESUS CHRIST USED THE MASORETIC TEXT OLD TESTAMENT!

The Preservation of the New Testament

Here are some New Testament passages which say that God will preserve His Word in the New Testament.

JESUS PROMISED
1) A COMPLETE, 2) SPIRIT-INSPIRED REVELATION,
3) THROUGH THE APOSTLES.

JOH 14:26 But **the Comforter, which is the Holy Ghost**, whom the Father will send in my name, **he shall teach <u>you</u> all <u>things</u>, and bring <u>all things</u> to <u>your</u> remembrance, <u>whatsoever</u> I have said unto <u>you</u>**.

JOH 15:26–27 But when **the Comforter** is come, **whom I will send unto <u>you</u>** from the Father, **even the Spirit of truth**, which proceedeth from the Father, he shall testify of me: 27 And **<u>ye</u> also shall bear witness**, because ye have been with me from the beginning.

JOH 16:12–15 I have yet many things to say unto you, but ye cannot bear them now. 13 Howbeit when he, **the Spirit of truth**, is come, **he will guide <u>you</u> into <u>all truth</u>**: for he shall not speak of himself; but whatsoever he shall hear, that shall he speak: and **he will shew <u>you</u> <u>things to come</u>**. 14 He shall glorify me: for he shall receive of mine, and shall shew it unto you. 15 All things that the Father hath are mine: therefore said I, that he shall take of mine, and shall shew it unto you.

In these three passages, observe the following statistics. Jesus says *9 times* that the complete revelation He is promising will be given to the Apostles—*not anybody else*. Jesus names the Holy Spirit *5 times* as the Bringer of all this Truth, thus confirming the coming of Inspired Scripture through the Apostles. Finally...*of supreme importance*...Jesus says at least *5 times* that this revelation would comprise "*All Things*"—*All things* Jesus ever told them during His ministry, *All Things* additional that He intended to reveal through Inscriptive Inspiration, and included therein *All Things* concerning prophesy of "things to come." Now, engage the old brain meat and *THINK*. These three passages *prove* that: Jesus promised 1) a complete, 2) Spirit-inspired revelation, 3) through the Apostles. NOBODY ELSE!

Consider the *logically undeniable inference* that shoots out from all this, jamming itself up your nose like a gorilla finger, 'til it bleeds:

ALL THE REVEALED SCRIPTURE THAT GOD, EVER AT ANY TIME, GAVE TO THE HUMAN RACE, STARTED WITH THE FIRST LETTER FROM MOSES' PEN AND ENDED WITH THE LAST PERIOD JOHN MADE IN REVELATION.

In other words—THE BIBLE...*ALL* OF THE BIBLE...*ONLY* THE BIBLE...IS REVEALED SCRIPTURE FROM GOD. For English speakers, that's The King James Bible (AV 1611). Moses began writing The Bible in 1491 BC, during Israel's Exodus from Egypt. John the Apostle wrote the last word of Revelation in 96 AD, during the life of Roman emperor Trajan. Since then, *EVERY* preacher, prophet, priest, pope, or pontificating pooh-bah, in *ALL* of the human race and history, in *ANY* religion real or imaginable, that claimed or claims or ever will claim that he/she/it (~~Bruce~~/Caitlyn Jenner type) brings *even one single inspired word from God*, IS A ***LIAR***. Proof? I just did. Read those 3 passages of Scripture one more time...then...read this:

> 1 John 5:10,20-21 He that believeth on the Son of God hath the witness in himself: **he that believeth not God hath made him a liar; because he believeth not the record that God gave of his Son**....20 And we know that **the Son of God is come, and hath given us an understanding**, that we may know him that is true, and we are in him that is true, even in **his Son Jesus Christ. <u>This is the true God, and eternal life.</u> 21 Little children, keep yourselves from idols**. Amen.

See?

JESUS PROMISED TO PRESERVE HIS WORDS.

LUK 21:33 Heaven and earth shall pass away: but **my words shall not pass away.**

JESUS PROMISED TO PUBLISH HIS WORDS WORLD-WIDE.

MAR 13:10 And the gospel must first be published among all nations.

> Note—85% of the translations of God's Word into foreign languages on the mission field has been done from the King James Version English! No other text type even remotely compares to this.

ACT 1:8 But ye shall receive power, after that the Holy Ghost is come upon you: and ye shall be witnesses unto me both **in Jerusalem, and in all Judaea, and in Samaria, and unto the uttermost part of the earth.**

Note—The spread of the King James type text after Samaria was into Antioch of Syria, Paul's home church; then from there all over the Roman Empire as a result of Paul's missionary journeys. Finally, it spread over Europe and the world, and comprises 85–95% of extant copies of the Greek New Testament. The Scholars' Text of the new revised bibles originated in Alexandria, Egypt and spread to Palestine, then to Rome, and comprises <5% of extant manuscripts.

ACT 2:1–8 And when **the day of Pentecost** was fully come, they were all with one accord in one place. 2 And suddenly there came a sound from heaven as of a rushing mighty wind, and it filled all the house where they were sitting. 3 And there appeared unto them cloven tongues like as of fire, and it sat upon each of them. 4 And they were all **filled with the Holy Ghost**, and **began to speak with other tongues[1]**, as the Spirit gave them utterance.

5 And there were dwelling at Jerusalem Jews, devout men, out of every nation under heaven. 6 Now when this was noised abroad, the multitude came together, and were confounded, because that **every man heard them speak in his own language[2]**. 7 And they were all amazed and marvelled, saying one to another, Behold, are not all these which speak Galilaeans? 8 And how hear we every man **in our own tongue[1], wherein we were born**?

[1] Gk. *glossa 1100* (Strong's Concordance, Gk. lexicon) = the tongue; by impl. a language.

[2] Gk. *dialektos 1258* = a (mode of) discourse, a dialect, a language.

Note—This is a prime Proof Text (we'll study what that is later) for both Inscriptive Inspiration which gives Scripture, and Understanding Inspiration which helps translate Scripture. This right here is what happened with the King James Translation Committee—God's Providence had put the Masoretic Hebrew and Textus Receptus Greek on the table before them (Inscriptive Inspiration and Understanding Inspiration), then God gave them Understanding Inspiration, just like on this Day of Pentecost, to help them translate it into English...*and did let none of His Words fall to the ground.*

JESUS SAID THE WORD WOULD BE KNOWN BY ITS FRUITS

MAT 7:15–20 **Beware of false prophets**, which come to you in sheep's clothing, but inwardly they are ravening wolves. 16 **Ye shall know them by their fruits**. Do men gather grapes of thorns, or figs of thistles? 17 Even so **every good tree bringeth forth good fruit**; but a corrupt tree bringeth forth evil fruit. 18 **A good tree cannot bring forth evil fruit, neither can a corrupt tree bring forth good fruit.** 19 Every tree that bringeth not forth good fruit is hewn down, and cast into the fire. 20 **Wherefore by their fruits ye shall know them.**

1TH 1:4–6 <u>Knowing, brethren beloved, your election of God.</u> 5 For **our gospel came** not **unto you** in word only, but also **in power, and in the Holy Ghost**, and in much assurance; as <u>ye know what manner of men we were among you for your sake.</u> 6 And **ye became followers of us, and of the Lord**, having received the word in much affliction, with joy of the Holy Ghost.

COL 1:5–6 For the hope which is laid up for you in heaven, whereof ye heard before in **the word of the truth of the gospel**; 6 Which is come unto you, as it is in all the world; and **<u>bringeth forth fruit, as it doth also in you</u>, since the day ye heard of it, and knew the grace of God in truth**:

Consider the Saints of the Old Testament, then study the Saints of the New Testament. *They bring forth the same fruits* of a Believing Heart and a Committed Life...*because they have The Same Book.* Now, consider all Believers who *sincerely and committedly* live their lives by a King James Bible, and compare them with the Old and New Testament Saints. *They bring forth the SAME fruits, because they have THE SAME BOOK.* As I have said so many times before, The Bible is *not* an ordinary book.

*****

Chapter 2—Basics of Bible Interpretation

Introduction
The 4 PRINCIPLES of Bible Study
The 5 RULES of Bible Study

Introduction

Just to clear our minds, then refocus, please review the description of Biblical Hermeneutics, on pages 4-7, called *For the rest....* Thank you.

I make an emphatic *distinction* between the 4 Principles and the 5 Rules of Bible Study. The Principles *govern* the Rules, and the Rules *apply* the Principles—and the two are *not* the same.

Consider using a map. One must do two things: First Orient the map, then Navigate with it, and the two are not the same. Orienting the map means to align it to true north (as opposed to magnetic north, which a compass indicates). On a proper map, there is a little chart in a corner that shows the angle of declination. Place the map on a flat surface with a compass on top, then rotate the map until the compass reading matches the declination. Now, you're ready to navigate. Without orienting first, the map could be utterly useless. Navigating then means first locating your present position on the map, then locating where you want to go, finally noting the proper compass reading in that direction...taking declination into account (or you might wander until you die amongst the giant trees).

The 4 Principles are sort of like map orienting, and the 5 Rules are like navigating. You must *orient* your mind and heart by those 4 Principles first, or the 5 Rules will lead you in circles. Once oriented, you must then *follow* those 5 Rules rigorously, or you're back into wandering in circles.

Finally, an apology. Socrates taught me, when I read Plato's Dialogues in high school, that a wise man knows nothing, and knows that he knows nothing. I hope I'm wise, for I sure don't know much. I have one advantage over Socrates—I have the Word of God...and God knows everything. All I have to do is read The Book. That's where my teachers showed me the 4 Principles and the 5 Rules. They didn't make that distinction, that's my contribution. My apology is, there may be more, maybe a whole lot more, than these 4 and 5...I just don't know, and I'm sorry for that and wish I had more for you. But, I do know this: There are *at least* 4 Principles, and there are *no less than* 5 Rules. So, I will show you what I know; and, I will show you how to use them. The Word of God is much like a Map of Destiny. Use it wisely—*as it is designed to be used*—pay careful attention to all the twists and turns, and though it be a hard and rigorous journey, you'll find your way through Life.

> Isa 35:8-10 And **an highway shall be there**, and a way, and it shall be called The way of holiness; the unclean shall not

pass over it; but it shall be for those: the wayfaring men, though fools, shall not err therein. 9 No lion shall be there, nor any ravenous beast shall go up thereon, it shall not be found there; but **the redeemed shall walk there**: 10 And **the ransomed of the LORD shall return**, and come to Zion with songs and everlasting joy upon their heads: they shall obtain joy and gladness, and sorrow and sighing shall flee away.

The 4 Principles of Bible Study

Let's begin by understanding what a Principle is.

> **principle.** *A* fundamental truth or proposition that serves as the foundation for a system of belief or behavior or for a chain of reasoning: *the basic principles of Christianity.* [Oxford American Dictionary]

As I said, The Principles *govern* the Rules, and the Rules *apply* the Principles—and the two are *not* the same. Keep this in mind, and let's look at those 4 Principles of Bible Study.

1. The Principles of Primary and Secondary Meanings

There are two approaches to use in dealing with the meaning of Bible words. *Either* one takes the Primary meanings most of the time and the Secondary meanings only when necessary, *Or* one takes the Secondary meanings most of the time and the Primary meanings only when necessary.

The Bible Method is

> *The Principle of Primary Meanings.*
>
> All Bible words are to be taken in their primary meanings unless a) the usage is obviously figurative, or b) the results are absurd or cause a contradiction between Scriptures; in the latter case, a secondary meaning is to be sought which agrees with other verses on the same topic using that word, or a synonym, in its primary meaning.

NEH 8:8,12 So they read in the book in the law of God **distinctly**[1], and **gave**[2] **the sense**[3], and caused them to understand the reading....12 And all the people went their way to eat, and to drink, and to send portions, and to make great mirth, because they had understood **the words**[4] that **were declared**[5] unto them.

> [1] Heb. *PaRaSH* 6567 (Strong's Heb. lexicon) = (1) To separate, to distinguish. (2) To declare distinctly, to define. (3) To expand, to spread out. Here a participle,

"They read 'spread-ing out' or 'distinguishing' (by implication, the words)."

2 Heb. *SooM* 7760 = To put, place, give (wide variety of meanings). Here an infinitive, "to give."

3 Heb. *SeKeL* 7922 = Understanding, sense, signification. Here in masculine singular, the form in Heb. for "the [noun]", the demonstrative singular. The meaning of the word is precisely as translated by the King James Version, "the sense," i.e., the primary meaning as opposed to all other 'senses' or secondary meanings.

4 Heb. *DaBaR* 1697 = Word. Answers to *logos* in Gk., the primary Heb. word for 'word'. It was not just the overall or general meaning of the passage that was explained; they were also given the meaning of *the individual words*!

5 Heb. *YaDHa'* 3045 = To know, to acquire knowledge; hence, to make to know.

This is the main Proof Text (I'll explain Proof Text in the next section) for the Principle of Primary Meanings. For now, Scan over Neh 8:7-9. Notice the names Ezra, Nehemiah, and Zechariah. These 3 men were inspired prophets who wrote Scripture. When you read Neh 8:8,12 never forget: *This is the way the Prophets who* wrote *Scripture* taught *Scripture*. They taught *literally, grammatically, and definitionally*...always using the Principle of Primary Meanings. The way I'm doing now, the way my teachers taught me, the way I'm teaching you.

Here are some more Proof Texts that teach the Principle of Primary Meanings.

> HAB 2:2 And the LORD answered me, and said, **Write the vision, and <u>make it plain</u> upon tables, that he may run that readeth it.**
>
>> NOTE that "readeth" is the primary verb and "may run" is the secondary verb conditioned upon the action of the primary verb. This implies primary meanings, which everyone is familiar with, so the runner doesn't have to stop and use a dictionary to figure out what the directions mean.
>
> EPH 3:3-4 How that by revelation he made known unto me the mystery; (as **I wrote afore in few words, 4 Whereby, when ye read, ye may understand** my knowledge in the mystery of Christ)

ACT 17:2-3 And Paul, as his manner was, went in unto them, and three sabbath days **reasoned with them out of the scriptures**, 3 **Opening** [to explain or define] **and alleging** [to produce as evidence, i.e., cited verses], that Christ must needs have suffered, and risen again from the dead; and that this Jesus, whom I preach unto you, is Christ.

2CO 1:13 For **we write none other things unto you, than what ye read or acknowledge** [Eng. "to know or recognize;" Gk. "to be fully acquainted with"]; and I trust ye shall acknowledge even to the end;

> NOTE—No hidden codes or mystical and occult meanings...it's all in plain language.

1CO 14:9-11 So likewise ye, except ye utter by the tongue **words easy to be understood**, how shall it be known what is spoken? for ye shall speak into the air. There are, it may be, so many kinds of voices in the world, and none of them is without **signification**. Therefore if I know not the **meaning** of the voice, I shall be unto him that speaketh a barbarian, and he that speaketh shall be a barbarian unto me.

★PRO 8:8-9 **All the words of my mouth** are in righteousness; there is nothing froward or perverse in them. 9 **They are all plain to him that understandeth, and right to them that find knowledge.**

Here are some Old Testament examples using Primary Meanings, that do that gorilla finger thing up your nose.

GEN 2:23 And Adam said, This is now bone of my bones, and flesh of my flesh: she shall be called **Woman**, because she was taken out of **Man**.

GEN 29:32—30:24 [The names of the children of Leah and Rachel are *all* given in primary meanings]

EXO 15:23 And when they came to Marah, they could not drink of **the waters of Marah**, for they were <u>bitter</u>: therefore the name of it was called Marah.

Here are some New Testament examples using Primary Meanings, that again do that gorilla finger thing up your nose. Hey, I said it twice 'cause you got 2 nostrils! All kidding aside, the technical term for Bible Interpretation is *hermeneutics*, which is derived from the Gr. word *hermeneuo*. The following verses are a complete listing of all verses in the New Testament using the word "interpretation" in *any* form with an example (11x altogether):

- Gk. *hermeneuo 2059* = To translate or interpret. (4x)

    JOH 1:38 Then Jesus turned, and saw them following, and saith unto them, What seek ye? They said unto him, **Rabbi**, (which is to say, **being interpreted, Master**,) where dwellest thou?

    JOH 1:42 And he brought him to Jesus. And when Jesus beheld him, he said, Thou art Simon the son of Jona: thou shalt be called **Cephas, which is by interpretation, A stone**.

    JOH 9:7 And said unto him, **Go**, wash in the pool of **Siloam, (which is by interpretation, Sent**.) He went his way therefore, and washed, and came seeing.

    HEB 7:2 To whom [**Melchisedec**] also Abraham gave a tenth part of all; **first being by interpretation King of righteousness, and after that also King of Salem, which is, King of peace**;

- Gk. *diermeneuo 1329* = To translate or interpret thoroughly. (1x)

    ACT 9:36 Now there was at Joppa a certain disciple named **Tabitha, which by interpretation is called Dorcas**: this woman was full of good works and almsdeeds which she did.

- Gk. *methermeneou 3177* = To explain over; to retranslate. (6x)

    MAT 1:23 Behold, a virgin shall be with child, and shall bring forth a son, and they shall call his name **Emmanuel, which being interpreted is, God with us.**

    MAR 5:41 And he took the damsel by the hand, and said unto her, **Talitha cumi; which is, being interpreted, Damsel, I say unto thee, arise.**

    MAR 15:22 And they bring him unto the place **Golgotha, which is, being interpreted, The place of a skull.**

    MAR 15:34 And at the ninth hour Jesus cried with a loud voice, saying, **Eloi, Eloi, lama sabachthani? which is, being interpreted, My God, my God, why hast thou forsaken me**?

    JOH 1:41 He first findeth his own brother Simon, and saith unto him, We have found **the Messias, which is, being interpreted, the Christ**.

ACT 4:36 And Joses, who by the apostles was surnamed **Barnabas, (which is, being interpreted, The son of consolation,)** a Levite, and of the country of Cyprus,

I think this whole subsection *proves beyond doubt* that **The Bible Method** is to use the Principle of Primary Meanings. You see, this is *not* "something Conrad Jarrell just made up."

However, there are *lots* of people that just *love* to make up bibley things. Consider **The Scholarly Method,**

The Principle of Secondary Meanings.

Use whatever Secondary Meanings for Bible Words that you prefer, or those which are needed to protect your denomination's doctrinal bias, or just whichever ones cover your tail best if you made a mistake which you would rather not admit.

Here's what Secondary Meanings comes down to:

a. In a college level dictionary, the average word has about 25 definitions listed; let's assume there are 5 definitions on average that would be pertinent in defining Bible words.

b. There are 31,173 verses in the Bible, and about 25 words in each verse.

c. Let's assume that of the 25 words in each verse, there are only 5 words about which there might be disagreement over meanings.

d. QUESTION 1: If we disagree about the meaning of only 5 words in the average Bible verse, and if we can narrow it down to only 5 definitions of each we disagree over, *how many versions of each verse* could we come up with, using the scholarly method of Secondary Meanings? ANSWER: 5^5 = **3,125 versions** *of each verse*!

e. QUESTION 2: Using the scholarly method, with 3,125 versions of each verse, *how many different Bible versions* could we come up with? ANSWER: $31,173^{3,125} = 10^{14,043}$ **bible versions**...that's a whole lot. To give you some idea of how big that number is, there are only 10^{79} electrons in the entire known universe; it would be possible to cram only 10^{130} electrons in if you smushed them belly button to backbone, like a bowl full of grits. Get the picture?

f. Let's assume that two people only disagree about one single word in each Bible verse (an obviously foolish assumption), and let's further assume that they disagree over only two definitions of that word (a downright asinine assumption).

QUESTION 3: How many *different Bible versions now* can they come up with?

ANSWER: $31,173^2 = 971,755,920$ versions.

In the last 103 years since 1881 (the first different scholarly version), there have been over 60+ scholarly versions published, or about one every 1.5 years.

QUESTION 4: How long will it take for the scholars to publish *all possible versions* using these very abbreviated assumptions?

ANSWER: About 1.5 billion years...*that's called "job security"*! And since they're all copyrighted...*lotsa money!*

g. On the other hand, by using the Principle of Primary Meanings, which results in only 1 meaning per verse, we would have only 1 Bible version in any language. *Surprise!* We have *only 1* in Hebrew—The Masoretic Text; we have *only 1* in Greek—The Textus Receptus; and we we have *only 1* in English—The King James Version (all as defined carefully in Chapter 1).

h. CONCLUSION: *The Scholars' Method of Secondary Meanings is butt-dumb.*

You see, from the facts above, that Secondary Meanings can be used to give *any* passage the *exact opposite* meaning of what it actually says using Primary Meanings; and thus, can give every single shade of meaning in between. Therefore, Secondary Meanings can be used to give *any* passage whatever, *any* meaning whatever, *regardless of what it actually says.* This is why professional Bible Scholars, who make a lot of money from tenured professorships and copyrights, *do so love* Secondary Meanings—they get paid to make up *any* bibley things they wish. And they can sell them for money. See?

Just for funsies...Where do you suppose the Principle of Secondary Meanings for Bible Words came from? Looky here:

> GEN 3:1-5 Now **THE SERPENT** was more subtil than any beast of the field which the LORD God had made. And he said unto the woman, **Yea, hath God said**, Ye shall not eat of **every** tree of the garden? [how about that? "The" really means "every"! COJ]
>
> 2 And the woman said unto the serpent, We may eat of the fruit of the trees of the garden: 3 But of the fruit of the tree which is in the midst of the garden, God hath said, Ye shall not eat of it, **neither** shall ye **touch** it [the gal learned fast, "dress and keep" really means the opposite "don't touch"! COJ], **lest** ye die [the gal learned double fast, "*surely* die" really means "*lest* ye die"! COJ].

4 And **THE SERPENT said** [a new and scholarly teacher, COJ] unto the woman, **Ye shall not surely die** ["*surely* die" *really* means the opposite "*not* surely die." Wow! Aren't Secondary Meanings preferred by scholars *neat*? COJ] : **5 For God doth know that in the day ye eat thereof, then your eyes shall be opened, and ye shall be as gods**, knowing good and evil [how's that for new doctrine that was *never there before*, just by changing a few *primary* meanings to *secondary* meanings...See? COJ].

Let's review, exactly, how Satan taught Eve to become the scholarly Head of the Translation Committee of the New Satanic Version...

Step 1) *Question* the Word of God.

Step 2) *Add* to the Word of God.

Step 3) *Deny* the Word of God.

Step 4) *Defy* the Word of God.

Step 5) *Use* any Secondary Meanings you wish.

...As my old Marine Corps Drill Instructor at Parris Island used to say, "That's aallll they are to it!"

CONCLUSION: Primary and Secondary Meanings

JOH 8:30-32 As he spake these words, many believed on him. **31 Then said Jesus to those Jews which believed on him**, If ye continue in my word, then are ye my disciples indeed; 32 And **ye shall know the truth, and the truth shall make you free**.

Now, of these two methods—Which makes you FREE?...and free of *WHAT*? Or should I ask...*WHOM*?

> This is why I put so much stress on the *Primary Meanings* of Bible words, and the *Grammar* and *Syntax* of Bible sentences. This is why, if you graduated from government schools since 1965, your head has been broken at the knees, because the government took away the 8 Parts of Speech, Sentence Diagraming, and Basic Logic. If *YOU* do not assume the responsibility of correcting this deficiency, you will remain a mental slug, worming your way slowly through the sludge of...*WordMud*.

2. THE PRINCIPLE OF PROOF TEXTS AND REFERENCE TEXTS

More definitions (in this book, they never stop coming).

> PROOF TEXT—A text that speaks *definitively* about some point of doctrine, it actually *says* it. Example:

EPH 1:3-7 Blessed be the God and Father of our Lord Jesus Christ, who hath blessed us with **all spiritual blessings** in heavenly places in Christ: 4 According as **he hath chosen us in him** <u>before the foundation of the world, that we should be holy and without blame before him in love</u>: 5 **Having predestinated us** <u>unto the adoption of children by Jesus Christ to himself, according to the good pleasure of his will, 6 To the praise of the glory of his grace</u>, wherein **he hath made us accepted** in the beloved. 7 In whom **we have redemption** <u>through his blood, the forgiveness of sins, according to the riches of his grace</u>;

You see the beauty of a Proof Text. A Proof Text *states* a point of doctrine so clearly and definitively that it needs little or no explanation. It means what it *says*, because it says what it *means*. The power of a Proof Text shines when some bonehead says, "Aw, that's just your interpretation." You can point out that no interpretation at all is involved—both of you *see* exactly what it *says*, and that is exactly what it *means*...and the problem is, *he doesn't believe it!*

REFERENCE TEXT—A text that *mentions* a point of doctrine in passing (*refers* to it), but does *not actually say* anything definitive about that point of doctrine. Example:

MAR 16:15-16 And he said unto them, Go ye into all the world, and preach the gospel to every creature. 16 He that believeth and is **baptized** [How? There are several baptisms taught in Scripture—the text doesn't *say*] **shall be saved** [Eternally or temporally?—the text doesn't *say*]; but he that believeth not shall be **damned** [Eternally or temporally?—the text doesn't *say*].

You see how trickery can use a Reference Text? Palming off a Reference text *as if* it were a Proof text allows a Professional Bible Scholar to *look like* he is stacking Scriptures a mile high, when virtually *no* verse he has quoted actually *says* the doctrine at all (**Piled high and Deep**...think about it). This is a tool of the trade for most popular Professional Bible Scholars. Now that you know how to spot it, keep your eyes open—you will see it in the most amazing places (Pro 14:6).

Proof Texts are fairly few in number, usually less than half a dozen or so on most doctrines; so it is relatively easy for most people to understand them and then use them in witnessing to others. For example, the Plan of Salvation can be presented and defended with about three dozen proof texts. Most erroneous proofs cite a Reference Text that does *not actually say* what you are then told it *means*. Review that Garden of Eden Thing again. Here are some warnings against this type of deception:

> EPH 4:11-14 And he gave some, apostles; and some, prophets; and some, evangelists; and some, pastors and teachers; 12 For the perfecting of the saints, for the work of the ministry, for the edifying of the body of Christ: 13 Till we all come in the unity of the faith, and of the knowledge of the Son of God, unto a perfect man, unto the measure of the stature of the fulness of Christ: 14 That we henceforth be no more children, tossed to and fro, and **carried about with every wind of doctrine, by the sleight of men, and cunning craftiness, whereby they lie in wait to deceive;**

> 2CO 4:1-2 Therefore seeing **we** have this ministry, as we have received mercy, we faint not; 2 But have **renounced the hidden things of dishonesty, not walking in craftiness, nor handling the word of God deceitfully;** [Paul had been a Jewish Professional Bible Scholar—he knew the trade] but by manifestation of the truth commending ourselves to every man's conscience in the sight of God.

> 2PE 3:15-16 And account that the longsuffering of our Lord is salvation; even as our beloved brother **Paul** also according to the wisdom given unto him **hath written unto you**; 16 As also in all his epistles, speaking in them of these things; in which are **some things hard to be understood, which they that are unlearned and unstable wrest, as they do also the other scriptures, unto their own destruction.**

This Reference Text trickery is especially effective the smaller the number of proof texts for a given doctrine (say, The Virgin Birth or The Trinity). A deceiver could use Secondary Meanings, along with carefully selected Reference Texts, to claim that those Proof Texts actually *mean* the opposite of what they *say* (much the way the Serpent did with Eve in the Garden of Eden). Then he can say, "Show me just one verse that says any different. Come on, just one." Of course, there aren't any more—he used all the Proof Texts there were...*as he explained them away.* It can be made to look so...Credibly Plausible. **P**iled **h**igh and **D**eep, remember?

3. THE PRINCIPLE OF TEXT GOVERNS CONTEXT

When studying The Bible, the Text *always* governs the Context.

Yep. More definitions. This is a lesson in itself: A word *says* it, the definition is what it *means*. See?

> **text.** 1. The actual structure of words in a piece of writing or printing; wording. 6. A Biblical passage quoted as authority for a belief or as the topic of a sermon.
>
> **context.** The parts of a sentence, paragraph, discourse, etc. that occur just before and after a specified word or passage, and determine its exact meaning: as, it is unfair to quote this remark out of its *context*.
>
> [Webster's New World Dictionary of the American Language]

A very important concept in Bible Study is the *relationship* between the Text and the Context. In ordinary books and everyday writing, the use of a Text *inside* of a Context can help determine the Text's exact meaning...*as it is being used in that Context*. This is because all words have many shades of meaning, and good writing brings out just the shade of meaning the writer is trying to put across. Good writing, like good speaking, is fluid—it flows as needed into the cracks and crevices of the moment, to convey an *idea* as seamlessly as possible. *Look* at the definition of Context again, and notice the phrase "and determine its exact meaning." See?

But, that is in ordinary writing...and The Bible is *not* an ordinary book. God (one of Whose names is *The Word*) frequently uses words whose definitions *are intended to shape the Context*. Go back to pp. 28-29 and read Neh 8:8,12 one more time...very carefully. Recall the Principle of Primary Meanings. When studying The Bible...and The Bible is *not* an ordinary book...the Text *always* governs the Context. Why is that? Ordinary writing, a part of ordinary communication, must flow through time, and thus adjust to changing circumstances. But, The Bible is *not* an ordinary book—God designed The Bible to have an eternal and unchanging message, no matter how much human circumstances change...so, the meaning of the words, the Text, remains fixed and unchanging, and thus determines Context, so the Message of The Bible (which is *not* an ordinary book) remains *unchanged* through all ages. There are 3 good reasons *why* this is so.

3 Reasons Why Text governs Context...IN BIBLE STUDY

1. THE HISTORICAL REASON—In 1611, when the King James Version was published, its text became, as it were, **frozen in time.** The 1611 Bible text has *not* grown and evolved—Its words have *not* accrued additional meanings *in Biblical usage,* and that is the key point. Add the

fact that the English language was essentially etymological from 1550-1650 (words carried the primary force of meaning), and the argument that the language of the King James Version is frozen in time becomes conclusive. For this reason alone, it should be obvious that text must govern context *when studying Bible passages.* Much the same argument can be made when studying the Hebrew *Masoretic Text* and the Greek *Textus Receptus.* Once the original autograph was written, those words become **frozen in time**; and God does let none of those words fall to the ground (1 Sam 3:19).

2. THE LOGICAL REASON—The Biblical context, by definition, is composed of nothing but Biblical text; and Biblical text, by definition, is composed of nothing but Biblical words. If it is argued that the ultimate meaning of the Biblical words is derived from the Biblical context, then a strange chain of reasoning is forced upon us:

> The individual Biblical words must be held to be ultimately meaningless until the Biblical context imparts meaning. Consequently, if that is true, then the Biblical text, being composed of so many ultimately meaningless Biblical words is also ultimately meaningless until the Biblical context imparts meaning. But then, the Biblical context itself is composed only of so much ultimately meaningless Biblical text, and therefore has no ultimate meaning, and thus can impart no ultimate meaning to the Biblical words.

Thus, the contrary argument reduces to absurdity, so is manifestly asinine. Therefore, Text *always* takes precedence over Context, *when interpreting Bible passages.*

3. THE BIBLICAL REASON—The Bible *says* so! Here is the Proof Text:

> PRO 25:11 A word **fitly**[1] spoken is like apples of gold in **pictures**[2] of silver.
>
> [1] An Hebrew phrase (composed of 5921 + 655, meaning literally "upon a season," in other words, "in due time, at an appropriate time."
>
> [2] Heb *MaSeKiYTH* 4906 = a carved figure, ie, a picture or picture frame.

The text is the 'apples of gold,' the context is the 'pictures of silver.' This cannot be denied, because the 'apples of gold' are said to be 'a word,' and the word is 'fitly spoken,' it 'fits into' what is spoken, ie, a context. Also, gold is valued more highly than silver. Therefore, the Bible declares that words, or Text, take precedence over Context—*when interpreting Bible passages.*

Well then, you might ask, What about the Bible Context? Here's all you need to know about the Context—Pay attention to **Who** is saying **What** to **Whom**, and **Why**, and **When**, and **Where**. Answer those six questions and you've pretty much got what's useful about the Context.

4. The Principle of Work from the Top Down

When studying Bible doctrine, always work down from the Greater to the Lesser, down from Eternal things to Timely, down from Heavenly things to Earthly.

- Always work down from the Greater to the Lesser—Proof Text:

> HEB 7:7 And <u>without all contradiction</u> **the less is blessed of the better.**

The context is Melchisedec blessing Abraham, when Abraham paid him tithes after the Battle of the Four Kings. Melchisedec was both a priest and a king, so outranked Abraham on both counts—the Less was blessed of the Better. The event is treated as an example of the general principle. Further, in Bible study, this general principle allows of no exceptions: "And <u>without all contradiction</u> the less is blessed of the better."

- Always work down from Eternal things to Timely—Proof Text:

> ROM 4:17 (As it is written, I have made thee a father of many nations,) before him whom he believed, even **God**, who quickeneth the dead, and **calleth those things which be not as though they were**.

God "worketh all things after the counsel of his own will" (EPH 1:11). In eternity past, He formulated an Eternal Plan. Now in Time, that Plan is unfolding, and will not admit of the slightest alteration. To understand things in Time, one *must* begin with that Eternal Plan. To understand the timely operations of the local church, for instance, it is necessary first to consider the Eternal Church, and how that pattern governs the timely.

- Always work down from Heavenly things to Earthly—Proof Text:

> MAT 6:10 Thy kingdom come. Thy will be done in earth, as it is in heaven.

The Lord Jesus Christ taught us to pray for these things. Observe that the pattern for all godly activities on earth is God's will and obedience thereto in heaven. It follows logically that, in order to perform God's will on earth, we must first consider that heavenly pattern:

> 2CO 4:18 While we **look not at the things which are seen, but at the things which are not seen**: for **the things which are seen are temporal**; but **the things which are not seen are eternal**.

There are 3 Reasons for the Principle of Work from the Top Down:

1. God has designed the world so that men *cannot* figure out heavenly things by reasoning *upward* to them:

   > ECC 3:11 He hath made every thing beautiful in his time: also he hath set the world in their heart, so that **no man can find out** the work that God maketh from the beginning to the end.

   > PSA 40:5 Many, O LORD my God, are **thy wonderful works** which thou hast done, and thy thoughts which are to us-ward: they **cannot be reckoned up in order unto thee**: if I would declare and speak of them, they are more than can be numbered.

   > NOTE—These two passages, taken together, *preclude* both Deductive and Inductive Reasoning...and there are no other *rational* methods. *Some* things we must be *told*.

2. Therefore, we *must* use heavenly things to fully understand earthly things:

   > HEB 9:23-24 It was therefore necessary that **the patterns of things in the heavens** should be purified with these; but **the heavenly things themselves** with better sacrifices than these. For Christ is not entered into **the holy places made with hands**, which **are the figures of the true**; but into heaven itself, now to appear in the presence of God for us:

   > EZE 43:8-11 In their setting of their threshold by my thresholds, and their post by my posts, and the wall between me and them, they have even defiled my holy name by their abominations that they have committed: wherefore I have consumed them in mine anger. Now let them put away their whoredom, and the carcases of their kings, far from me, and I will dwell in the midst of them for ever. Thou son of man,

shew the house to the house of Israel, that they may be ashamed of their iniquities: and **let them measure the pattern.** And if they be ashamed of all that they have done, shew them the form of the house, and the fashion thereof, and the goings out thereof, and the comings in thereof, and all the forms thereof, and all the ordinances thereof, and all the forms thereof, and all the laws thereof: and **write it in their sight, that they may keep the whole form thereof, and all the ordinances thereof, and do them.**

1CO 2:12-13 <u>Now we have received,</u> **not the spirit of the world, but the spirit which is of God**; that we might know the things that are freely given to us of God. Which things also we speak, **not in the words which man's wisdom teacheth, but which the Holy Ghost teacheth**; comparing spiritual things with spiritual.

NOTE—Things on this earth are reflections of things in heaven, when there is a relationship between them. Every *earthly* item in the service of God is a pattern, or figure, of some *heavenly* counterpart, which is itself the ultimate reality. Worldly men consider earthly things of primary importance, thus often wind up embracing earthly *delusions* and denying heavenly *realities*.

3. God will punish those who misuse His Word *differently*:

JOB 5:12-14 **He disappointeth the devices of the crafty**, so that their hands cannot perform their enterprise. **He taketh the wise in their own craftiness**: and **the counsel of the froward is carried headlong**. They meet with darkness in the daytime, and grope in the noonday as in the night.

NOTE—When people, even intelligent and educated people, start dabbling with God's Word, violating His own principles and rules for handling It, and perverting Its purpose for their own egotistic ends, God will simply turn their lights out...literally. They will become blind stumblebums, fumbling with something they no longer understand and can no longer explain. God just **P**iles it on, really **h**igh and really **D**eep.

"Church doctors? Church *doctors*? They ought to be called Church *babies*!" —Martin Luther

As we conclude this section, I remind you again of a distinction which I think so important. These 4 PRINCIPLES are like *Orienting* a map; the 5 RULES which follow are like *Navigating* with a map. Unless the map is oriented first, any navigating you attempt will most likely lead you in circles. Lastly remember, The Principles *govern* the use of the Rules, and the Rules *apply* the Principles.

The 5 Rules of Bible Study

These explanations will not attempt to be exhaustive. Rather, these are the *absolutely essential* Rules which *must* be followed in successful Bible study—they are Rules which God Himself, in His Book, has laid out for us to follow. All other rules—such as different figures of speech, the historical approach, the chronological approach, etc.—are good and useful in their way. But *these* five are not rules that men have made up to aid themselves, but Rules that The Bible Itself gives for the study of Itself. Such Rules men ignore at their peril.

There seem to be *at least* five such Rules, of *absolutely* universal application to *every* instance of Bible study, by their very nature allowing of *not one single exception* or suspension. These are not rules "that Conrad just made up." These are the very Rules of God governing Bible study, and I shall prove it as I was taught it...verse by verse. Here's a start. Christ taught that people must follow God's instructions, in order to understand the Bible.

> JOH 7:16-17 Jesus answered them, and said, My doctrine is not mine, but his that sent me. 17 **If any man will do his will, he shall know of the doctrine**, whether it be of God, or whether I speak of myself.

Christ plainly said that, in order to know God's doctrine (and why else, pray tell, do we study the Bible?), we must *do* God's will. The Greek is even stronger. The verb "do" is an infinitive: "If any man will to do His will..." The Bible student must make a strong commitment *to do* God's known will *before* any fruit can be expected from Bible study. Since God has most definitely made His will known regarding *how* we are to study His Book, anyone not willing *to do* God's will concerning Bible study is unlikely to either understand God's doctrine, or be able to defend it.

Let's segue right into it with a word about Apparent Contradictions. Most people attempt to solve apparent contradictions by VERSE-BANGING, opposing one passage to another, as if one part of the Bible will cancel or out-vote another part. The proper approach is VERSE- FITTING, finding out how *apparently* contradictory verses *actually fit* together. Generally speaking, if you start with a clear understanding of the 4 Principles we have studied, and carefully apply them using the 5 Rules below, you will almost never run into an apparent contradiction. Both the many *seeming* contradictions that folks will throw at you, and the few that you come across, will melt away with the careful application of these Biblical methods of Bible Study. Let's see how.

RULE #1—THERE IS NO CONTRADICTION IN THE BIBLE

> 2PE 1:20 **Knowing this first,** that **no** prophecy of the scripture is of any **private** interpretation.
>
> **private**. [from *privare*, to separate, deprive; from *privus*, separate, peculiar] Separate or apart.
>
> Greek *idios 2398* = private or separate.

The Primary Meaning of "private" (notice how Principle *governs* Rule) emphasizes one thing or group of things *as apart from* any or all other things. Since a prophecy is a divine utterance, and since Scripture is composed 100% of divine utterances (2TI 3:16), it is undeniable that this verse is *saying* plainly (and therefore plainly *means*) that no interpretation of any verse or group of verses stands apart from the interpretation of any or all other verses—*no exceptions*. A contradiction is a condition in which things tend to be contrary to each other. A contradiction in Scripture would mean that the interpretation of one or more verses is found to be *contrary* to the interpretation of some or all other verses. However, this condition is plainly stated by 2PE 1:20 to be impossible, with no exceptions allowed. Therefore, there is no contradiction in The Bible...only *apparent* contradictions exist, and exist *only* in our heads (notice how Rule *applies* Principle). And of course, on the bottom of our shoes, where we stepped in it. So, wipe that contradictory stuff off on the grass, and let's move on.

Let us see how this Rule #1 works, applied to the number one bedrock doctrine for Jews and Christians alike, what the Jews call the *Shama*.

> Deut 6:4-5 Hear (*Shama* H8085), O Israel: The LORD our God is one LORD: 5 And thou shalt love the LORD thy God with all thine heart, and with all thy soul, and with all thy might.
>
> *Shama Yisrael, Yehovah Elohainoo, Yehovah echad.*
>
> Hear, O Israel, Jehovah our God,   Jehovah is one.
>
> Mark 12:28-30 And one of the scribes came, and having heard them reasoning together, and perceiving that he had answered them well, asked him, Which is the first commandment of all? 29 And <u>Jesus answered him</u>, The first of

all the commandments is, **Hear, O Israel; The Lord our God is one Lord**: 30 And thou shalt love the Lord thy God with all thy heart, and with all thy soul, and with all thy mind, and with all thy strength: this is the first commandment.

Now, let us see how this *appears* to contradict with the number two bedrock doctrine for Christians, The Trinity (when a Jew hears this one, he staggers back in shock and crosses himself, before he realizes what he is doing!):

1 John 5:7 For **there are three** that bear record in heaven, the Father, the Word, and the Holy Ghost: and **these three are one**.

When Muslim or a Buddhist hears this, he shouts Whoa! and staggers back asking, How can *one* God be *three*?

Just remember, this is an *apparent* contradiction that exists *only* in our heads, not in Scripture (also on the shoes...step carefully). Let's work it out, using the Principle of Primary Meanings and the #1 Rule, There is no Contradiction in The Bible.

First, go back to the *Shama*. Now, notice two words: "God" and "one". Finally, observe that "God" in Heb is *Elohainoo* (plural possessive), and "one" in Heb is *echad*. Why is this important? Because we first need to be sure what The Bible *says*, before we declare what It *means*...because It *means* what It *says*.

"OK," you respond in frustration, "The Bible says *Elohainoo* and *echad*, so then what do those words *mean*?" So glad you asked, because this is sweet. First, here is a literal and *definitional* translation of the *Shama*:

> **Hear**-intelligently-and-obediently, O Israel, The-eternally-Self-existent-One, **our At-least-three-Mighty-Ones**, The-eternally-Self-existent-One is **united-into-One**.
>
> *Elohainoo* means "our At-least-three-Mighty-Ones".
> *echad* means "united-into-One".

As Einstein said, Let's keep this as simple as possible, but not any simpler. First, *Elohim* H430 = plural, <u>The</u> *at-least-three-Mighty-Ones*. When used of God Himself, this name is *always* plural (in Hebrew, plural is *three* or more). Furthermore, when referring to God Himself (as opposed to pagan gods), it *always* takes a *singular* verb (indicating just and only One). It appears thusly over 3,000 times in the OT. This name of God *implies* a unique three-in-one quality about God's Nature—A *Oneness* based upon the unvarying *singularity* of the associated verbs, and a *Threeness* based upon the obvious Hebrew plural. What really drives this point home is that this is *pre-*

cisely the way God Himself spoke these *exact* words to Moses, and this is *exactly* the way Moses himself *precisely* wrote these *exact* words down. Second, *echad* H259 = properly, "united," that is, "one." It comes from *achad* H258, perhaps a primitive root, = "to unify." *Echad* appears 885 times in the Old Testament, 684 times translated "one." Most of the other 201 times, it is translated variously, but in ways that state or imply oneness, unity, or harmonious agreement. But, I emphasize, when looked at etymologically, with consideration for its derivation, the Primary Meaning of *echad* is UNITED-INTO-ONE. There are <u>at least 8 verses</u> where this primary concept of *"echad =* united-into-one" is the obvious, grammatical, and logical meaning, apart from any and all other secondary meanings: The *Shama* Deut 6:4; Ezra 2:64; 3:9; 6:20; Ecc 11:6; Isa 65:25; Jdg 20:8; and 1 Sam 11:7. Arguably, there are more, but these are undeniable. This was the "not any simpler" part.

Now, here's the "simple" part—Grab ahold of something solid... this is gonna be deeeeep!—"Our At-least-three-Mighty-Ones", to keep it simple, are "united-into-One" God. *Exactly* as I John 5:7 *says,* "For **there are three** that bear record in heaven, the Father, the Word, and the Holy Ghost: and **these three are one**."

GOD IS A TRINITY—Three divine *Personalities* cohering in one single undivided divine *Nature.* Remember, these *exact* words that form The *Shama* were spoken by an *Infinite* Being explaining His Nature to *finite* beings. I suggest we follow Clint Eastwood's Dirty Harry Principle—"A man's got to know his limitations." Beyond a certain point, Either you *believe* what The Infinite Being *said...*Or you *don't.* It's just that simple.

The sad part is, although God spoke these *exact* words to Moses, and Moses wrote them down *exactly*—and God did let none of these words fall to the ground—the Jews who *understand* them exactly, do not *obey* them. Google around on the 'net, using the words *Elohim* and *echad.* You will find places where Jewish scholars *define the words precisely,* but then *interpret the meaning differently,* denying any trinitarian interpretation assiduously. They *hear* intelligently, but *not* obediently—they will not *Shama* (**Hear**-intelligently-**and**-obediently). See? The Jews have QUOTED the *Shama* religiously for 3500 years, but except for a faithful handful they have refused to OBEY. On the doctrine of God, the average Jew is as butt-headed as the average Muslim. They will both *agree* that He is the God of Abraham, but they will both *deny* that He is actually ECHAD—Sad, but true.

Thankfully, Kind Reader, now you *know* better...because now you *know* The Bible *means* what It *says*—and It *says* ECHAD. The bottom line is, when all these parallel verses are compared (the next Rule we will study), and all the Primary Meanings are considered and allowed to *govern*, then just as Rule #1 says, There are no Contradictions in The Bible. This is how Rule #1 works.

> RULE #2—COMPARE ALL CROSS-REFERENCES OR PARALLEL PASSAGES ON A GIVEN TOPIC.
>
> 1Co 2:13 Which things also we speak, not in **the words** which man's wisdom teacheth, but **which the Holy Ghost teacheth;** <u>comparing</u> **spiritual things with spiritual**.
>
> Rom 12:6 Having then gifts differing according to the grace that is given to us, whether prophecy, let us **prophesy according to the** <u>proportion</u> **of faith;**
>
>> **proportion**. 3. an harmonious relationship between parts or things; balance or symmetry. 6. [Rare], relation, other than quantity, between things; comparison; analogy.
>>
>> Gk. *analogia 356* = proportion; analogy, the right relation, the coincidence or agreement existing or demanded according to the standard of the several relations; not agreement as equality.

That first Proof Text of Rule #2 (see why I put a difference between Principles and Rules?) makes it very clear that the fundamental data of proper Bible Study is Bible Words. Bible Words in one passage are to be *compared* with how those key words or topics are used in other Bible passages. Look at the second Proof Text. 'Prophesy' means literally "to speak forth" (there those Principles are, governing Rules again; see the difference?). When we 'speak forth' Bible Words, we first carefully compare those Words with how they (or the same topic) were used in other Bible passages; then, we should 'speak forth' those Words *in the same way*—which is what 'analogy' means. When you read what The Bible *says*, then follow these Principles and Rules to understand what they *mean*, then your explanation of them *should say the same thing*. See?

I use commentaries, and I have a half dozen extremely good ones, but my first and foremost commentary, on *any* Bible passage, is *other* Bible passages using the same key words or topics. *After* I thus read God's comments on His Word, *then* I may read other people's comments (or not). Done correctly, as I am showing you, it is surprising how rarely you need to read those other comments. I mean, *There* it is, in God's Own Words. Who else's opinion could *possibly* be better?

My wife and I were at a Bible conference one time, I was up preaching and she was in the audience. She told me she overheard the fellow sitting behind her say to another guy, "I don't see why they think he's an interesting preacher...he's only *reading* verses that *say* it." Well, *Duuhh*.

Thing is, there are a lot of topics, and individual word usages, that are talked about a lot in The Bible. The Name of God, *Elohim*, appears over 3000 times in Scripture. The Name LORD appears over 6000 times. The word 'baptize' and its various cognates appears over 130 times in the New Testament. Trust me, it takes a while to compare those many passages properly. That's why God gave his people pastors; so folks can work and make a good living for their families, then sit in church on Sunday and listen for an hour, to what it took the man of God hours and hours and some time days to study out for their benefit.

One of the things that can shorten this grunt time somewhat, is how the Principle of Primary Meanings and the Principle of Proof Texts, together governing the Rule of Parallel Passages, can sometimes focus time way down. To see how all this works, let's consider the topic (or Doctrine) of Virgin Birth. Thankfully, there are only four Proof Texts that actually *say* it (or parts of it) definitively; only four, in the whole Bible. Since these Proof Texts are all teaching the Virgin Birth (or essential parts of it), they are also Parallel Texts. So, let's *compare* all these parallel passages, see how they are *analogous*, and thus composite the Doctrine of the Virgin Birth. Here are the texts:

> Gen 3:14-15 And the LORD God said unto the serpent, Because thou hast done this, thou art cursed above all cattle, and above every beast of the field; upon thy belly shalt thou go, and dust shalt thou eat all the days of thy life: 15 And I will put enmity between thee and the woman, and between thy seed and **her seed**; it shall bruise thy head, and thou shalt bruise **his heel**.

> Isa 7:14 Therefore the Lord himself shall give you a sign; Behold, **a virgin shall conceive**, and bear a son, and shall call his name Immanuel.

> Luk 1:26-35 And in the sixth month the angel Gabriel was sent from God unto a city of Galilee, named Nazareth, 27 To a virgin espoused to a man whose name was Joseph, of the house of David; and the virgin's name was Mary. 28 And the angel came in unto her, and said, Hail, thou that art highly favoured, the Lord is with thee: blessed art thou among women.
>   29 And when she saw him, she was troubled at his saying, and cast in her mind what manner of salutation this should be. 30 And the angel said unto her, Fear not, Mary: for thou hast found favour with God. 31 And, behold, **thou**

> shalt **conceive in thy womb**, and bring forth a son, and shalt call his name JESUS. 32 He shall be great, and shall be called **the Son of the Highest**: and the Lord God shall give unto him the throne of his father David: 33 And he shall reign over the house of Jacob for ever; and of his kingdom there shall be no end.
>
> 34 Then said Mary unto the angel, **How shall this be, seeing I know not a man?** 35 And the angel answered and said unto her, **The Holy Ghost shall come upon thee, and the power of the Highest shall overshadow thee: therefore also that holy thing which shall be born of thee shall be called the Son of God.**
>
> Matt 1:18-25 Now the birth of Jesus Christ was on this wise: When as his mother Mary was espoused to Joseph, before they came together, **she was found with child of the Holy Ghost.** 19 Then Joseph her husband, being a just man, and not willing to make her a public example, was minded to put her away privily.
>
> 20 But while he thought on these things, behold, the angel of the Lord appeared unto him in a dream, saying, Joseph, thou son of David, fear not to take unto thee Mary thy wife: for **that which is conceived in her is of the Holy Ghost. 21 And she shall bring forth a son, and thou shalt call his name JESUS: for he shall save his people from their sins**.
>
> 22 Now all this was done, that it might be fulfilled which was spoken of the Lord by the prophet, saying, 23 **Behold, a virgin shall be with child, and shall bring forth a son, and they shall call his name Emmanuel, which being interpreted is, God with us.**
>
> 24 Then Joseph being raised from sleep did as the angel of the Lord had bidden him, and took unto him his wife: 25 And knew her not till she had brought forth her firstborn son: and he called his name JESUS.

Interestingly enough, it turns out that the easiest way to do our comparison is chronologically, the same way God gave the Words (trust me, it is not often this easy). So, let's start with Genesis 3.

The key words for us to compare (with elsewhere) are **her seed** and **His heel**. First, these words tell us, undeniably, that somewhere way down the long years of that chosen bloodline, there is going to come...The Son. Second, we see that, in some way undefined here, Satan is going to seriously damage The Son's ability to...*walk* (how about Crucifixion and Death?—and we learn elsewhere, *then* He *walks* out of the grave!). Also, in some undefined way, The Son is going to seriously damage Satan in the head (how about Total Defeat of every ambition, then Eternal Damnation?).

There is something else...*hidden here!*...and not revealed until over 4000 years later. Primary Meanings, now...what does **her seed** *actually say* in Hebrew? The *secondary* meaning is exactly what everybody read for those 4000 years: 'her descendant,' her bloodline child. And of course, that is *exactly* what it *meant*. But, you see, *there is more!* Again, what is the *Primary* Meaning of **her seed**? You ready for this? According to Thayer's *Greek-English Lexicon*, Heb. *zera'* H2233 literally means "her *semen virile.*" Check out this Parallel Passage, and notice how the Primary Meaning *governs*:

> Lev 15:16-18 And if any man's **seed** (H2233) of copulation go out from him, then he shall wash all his flesh in water, and be unclean until the even. 17 And every garment, and every skin, whereon is the **seed** (H2233) of copulation, shall be washed with water, and be unclean until the even. 18 The woman also with whom man shall lie with **seed** (H2233) of copulation, they shall both bathe themselves in water, and be unclean until the even.

See how the definition of words, taken Scripture with Scripture, show us clearly that The Bible *means* what It *says*?

The unavoidable implication is, She will somehow, in some unexplained way, produce a *seed* that will fertilize her egg, and produce The Son! God then waited over 3300 years, before giving us a clue in Isaiah, and over 4000 years before letting Matthew and Luke explain it, so we are going to wait a few more paragraphs then let them tell it.

So this brings us to the Parallel Passage in Isaiah, "A **virgin** (*'almah* H5959) shall **conceive**". The Primary Meaning of this word is "virgin." It comes from a root which means, "veiled, or private." The secondary meaning is, "a young woman." It is almost exactly equal to the English word "maiden;" which means primarily "a virgin," secondarily "a young woman." The proof of virginity, in English, is called "*maiden*head." In Heb, *'almah* implies *veiled*. Taken in Primary Meanings, comparing Parallel Verses, the Scripture *cannot possibly* be misunderstood—God has given us a sign (i.e., He *did* it), somehow, in some unexplained way, a Virgin will produce a *seed* that fertilizes her egg, and then she will birth The Son! Let me say this very plainly and emphatically: *Anybody*...Ph.D., Th.D., D.D., or whatever...that tells you the King James Bible mistranslated "virgin," and it *really means* "young woman," is at least an *ignoramus* and at worst a *liar*, who is trying to kick your head around like a soccer ball. You should walk away and never look back.

Walk all the way over to Luke and Matthew and see how they explain it. Luke (told by an angel) and Matthew (inspired by the Holy Ghost) testify that *God <u>caused</u> Mary to <u>conceive</u> in her womb*. Revelation does not specify exactly how, but logic and the meaning of words leave little to the imagination. In her womb was found a male seed, and it combined with her egg—which is *exactly* what "conceive" means in these circumstances, and *nothing* else—and The Son was born. How? we may legitimately ask; and logic and the precise meaning of words answer: When one of her cells was dividing to produce two eggs, if God altered the Y chromosome of one half to an X chromosome (thus producing the *essence* of a sperm cell), then *reversed* the cell division *before the cell wall divided*, that would thus cause the Virgin (who had not known a man) to *literally* conceive—*and every single atom involved would have been produced by her body... so was <u>Her</u> seed*.

Primary Meanings and Proof Texts *governing* Parallel Passages, The Word of God in the Words of God, of which for over 4000 years He did let none fall to the ground. The Bible, you see, is *not* an ordinary book.

> RULE #3—THE BIBLE IS A COMPLETED REVELATION,
> SO THE ARGUMENT FROM SILENCE IS VALID; I.E.,
> IF IT IS NOT IN THE BIBLE, IT IS NOT BIBLICAL.

HEB 7:14 For it is evident that our Lord sprang out of Juda; **of which tribe Moses spake nothing** concerning priesthood.

The Argument from Silence is generally considered a logical fallacy; as when a Ph.D. in a Harvard philosophy class affirms, "It's never, ever, happened before; *therefore* it will never, ever happen (while denying Creation);" then immediately drops dead of a fatal heart attack (which of course had never, ever, happened to him before).

Many, many times throughout history, and *especially* today, people have advocated the idea that, if something is not *specifically forbidden* in The Bible, then it must be...'okay'. Now, let me show you the hammer upside the head, that brains this stupid idea: The Bible many times condemns *Supersets* of different stuff, and thus *logically* condemns all *Subsets* therein...*without ever having to mention them specifically*. For example, *nowhere* in The Bible does it *specifically say* one cannot kill an unwanted baby by slashing it to pieces with a knife. But, one of the Ten Commandments *does* say, Thou shalt not kill (lit. Heb., *murder*)—a Superset that includes all Subsets, including using a scalpel to slice an unwanted baby to pieces in its mother's womb (Eng., *abortion*). See?

> **superset**. a set that includes another set or sets.
>
> **subset**. a part of a larger group of related things.
>
> [Oxford American Dictionary]

In this way, *every* stupid quasi-biblical argument *ever* made, trying to use the Argument from Silence ("It don't say nuthin' about that...") is brained by that hammer. Why? Because The Bible is a *completed* Revelation, which contains Supersets of different stuff, *and therefore logically applies everything God ever did say Scripturally to all that relevant Subset stuff*. And that means, that the Argument from Silence is valid...*when using Scripture!* The Bible is *not* an ordinary book. See?

Let's take another example: ~~Bruce~~/Caitlyn Jenner, the ~~former-man~~/now-'woman'. Anything in The Bible about a "gender sex change"? I never read it. Anything in The Bible about an operation to change a guy-face into a girly-face? Can't seem to find it. What does The Bible say about a guy getting plastic breast implants? Not in any English, Greek, or Hebrew concordance I've got, and I've got the best. What does The Bible say about a 'woman' with a guy's wee-wee? Or, for that matter, a 'guy' with a woman's woo-woo? Those topics seem to be missing from all 31,173 Bible verses in both the King James Bible and the underlying Hebrew and Greek texts as well...maybe it's in one of those Roman Catholic manuscripts—everything else seems to be. Well, 'if The Bible don't say nuthin' about none of that', do you suppose it might, somehow, be 'biblical'? If we took a poll from all those ordained lesbian preachers and those ordained queer preachers, especially the ones who have been to graduate school and have one of those fancy degrees...How many Bible verses might they give us? From what bibles, you reckon? Absolute fact—there won't be a single verse from a King James Bible...*because there aren't any*. Tell you what. Let's just chuck all that crapola, and see what The Bible *does* say about...*different Stuff*...like *That*. You know...Superset *Stuff*...that logically includes everything *imaginable* about... Subset *Stuff*, like *That*.

Let's go for some good Proof Texts, that flat *say* it. We will do fine with just two (but remember, there are more...*lots* more):

> Deu 22:5 The woman shall not wear that which pertaineth unto a man, neither shall a man put on a woman's garment: for **all that do so are abomination unto the LORD thy God**.
>
> Rom 1:26-27 For this cause God gave them up unto **vile affections**: for even their **women** did change **the natural use** into **that which is against nature**: 27 And **likewise also the men**, leaving **the natural use of the woman,**

burned in their lust one toward another; **men with men** working that which is unseemly, and receiving in themselves that recompense of their error which was meet.

Consider Deu 22:5. Can you say "Cross-dress"? *I knew you could!* The Oxford American Dictionary defines Cross-dress as "wear clothing typical of the opposite sex." You see The Problem? You *don't*? Then let me give you two examples.

First example, ~~Bruce~~/Caitlyn Jenner, the ~~former-man~~/ now-'woman'. When ~~he~~/she was a he, he decided he wanted to be a woman. Part of what he did to turn into a 'woman' was put on girly clothes and lipstick, cross-dressing. *Now*, we are told by the news media and the courts, ~~he~~/she is a 'woman'; even though ~~he~~/she has a guy's wee-wee, which is genuine because he/~~she~~ used it to father children. See?

Second example. The boy we all heard about in the news media (supported by the courts), who decided when he was little that he wanted to be a girl, so ~~he~~/she started cross-dressing and became a 'girl'. Now ~~he~~/she is allowed in school to use the girls' restroom, because ~~he~~/she is a 'girl' because ~~he~~/she wears a dress and says so. Now, ~~he~~/she can let the other girls watch ~~him~~/her wee-wee with ~~his~~/ her wee-wee, and ~~he~~/she can watch the other girls wee-wee with their woo-woos. See?

Now...do you see The Problem? You're *kidding*! OK then, let me spell it out. If cross-dressing, wearing clothing typical of the opposite sex, is part of what makes one the opposite sex (and the news media and the courts say so), then *exactly what is* "clothing typical of the opposite sex"? Think about it. If a guy/girl puts on a dress/pants, and THAT MAKES THEM a girl/guy, then *they are <u>actually</u> wearing clothing of the <u>same</u> sex <u>and</u> the <u>opposite</u> sex <u>at the same time!</u>* Logically then, since clothing is what makes the difference (and the news media and the courts say so), then the guy/girl is also a girl/guy *at the same time*...BUT—and here's The Problem—*their wee-wee/woo-woo <u>never changed</u>!*

Why all this confusion? Because way back in the '60s, the government took the 8 Parts of Speech, Sentence Diagramming, and Basic Logic out of the government school curriculum (review Brain Crutch, pp. 10-11). The government gave us Outcome-based Education, *and this is the butt-dumb stupid Outcome*—increasing numbers of children and adults who think that clothing and makeup determine gender more than wee-wees and woo-woos...*and the news media and the courts say so* (they also say Evolution happened, but *all* the missing links are...*missing*).

What does The Bible say? "**All that do so** [i.e., cross-dressing] **are abomination** unto the LORD thy God." Notice 2 things. **1)** The Bible says *nothing specific* about any details whatsoever, and yet DEFINES *everything imaginable* about any *conceivable* form of Cross-dressing in all *possible* cultures as an ABOMINATION to God. In other words, to paraphrase Heb 7:14, "Of which things The Bible spake nothing concerning permissibility." Supersets and Subsets...See? **2)** On Judgement Day, when God judges the souls and works of men and women *using The Bible* (Rev 20:12; Rom 2:16), for all the cross-dressed girly guys with wee-wees and guyly girls with woo-woos, it is not going to go well.

Can you say, "Homosexual"? *I knew you could!* The Oxford American Dictionary defines Homosexual as "a person who is sexually attracted to people of their own sex." That is *exactly* what Rom 1:26-27 is all about. This is one of those Proof Texts—it *says* it. Not only that, it is also an Argument from Silence text—everything it *doesn't* say in all the *conceivable* Subsets is LOGICALLY INCLUDED in what the Superset *does* say. Read those two verses very carefully, *paying close attention to the underlined words*. Let's start with **likewise**. It's one of those 'flip' things...*everything* said about *either* one applies *exactly* to the *other* one...see? No wiggle room at all. Next, consider **against nature**. On the one hand, we could *opinionate* about that all day: Harvard Ph.D.s could write papers, the Nobel committee could hand out peace prizes, lesbians and queers could march naked down main street waving signs, and the Supreme Court could issue a couple of decisions. OR...on the *other* hand...we could just use *one word*. Let's do that. Here it is: DNA. Whoa! Stagger back. We all know what *that* means, and there is no *opinion* to it. It is the coded information designed into all living things by the Creator at the time of Creation. Someone might object and insist, "I don't believe in creators and creation. All living things have evolved from primordial muck." Interestingly, that would make humans Muck People; and that *might* explain why, throughout history, people have always Mucked things up. But, let's stick to the point. Evolutionists *imagine* that it takes about 500 stages for one living thing to evolve into a different living thing. Fact is, there are over 200,000 different living thing fossils in the museums. Multiply imagination and fact together and you get *100 million*. Another fact: *Every single one of those 100 million missing link fossils is...MISSING*. If evolution happened, every one of those missing link fossils *should* be lying in the museums right beside the living thing fossils they supposedly produced. They are *not*. Because it didn't *happen* that way. It was *made* that way. Therefore, DNA is the coded information designed into all living things by the Creator at the time of Creation. It defines Life itself, as well as all of the actual multiplicity of possible specificities in which Life manifests as the living part of...NATURE. DNA may be thought of as the conceptual

Superset which is *reified* (look that word up, I'm teaching you...do it *now*, or I'll whang your knuckles with this ruler) into all living Subsets. Example: The Superset of Male and Female. Now, specifically, the Subset of *human* male and female. The way Nature works (following DNA instructions) with human males and females is: Males have wee-wees, females have woo-woos; wee-wees and woo-woos *naturally* fit together; when done as *Nature* was obviously designed to work, babies grow in female tummies, and come out through the woo-woo. That is Nature, which simply follows DNA instruction code. For queers to use their wee-wees on each other, or **likewise** for lesbians to use their woo-woos together, is **against nature**. And that is a boo-boo. Here are two more undeniable facts: 1) No lesbian ever made a baby in another lesbian's tummy; and, 2) No queer ever had a baby come out of his bummy. Nature does not work *That* Way.

Some Ph.D. from the Harvard Psychology Department might disagree. "You are forgetting True Love. If queers and lesbians *Truly Love* one another, that makes it all right. You're a Christian...don't you believe God is Love, as Jesus said? If homosexuals fulfill *True Love* with one another, aren't they manifesting what you call God in their relationship?" You had to go to a government school, *without* the 8 Parts of Speech, Sentence Diagramming, or Basic Logic to buy that load of crap. Just stick with a King James Bible, and observe that It *says*, "**Burned in their lust** one toward another". Yes, Dear Reader, that is another Superset, and it logically covers *all* Subsets. The Word of God SAYS, in The Words of God, **burned in their lust**. What does that MEAN? *Every* possible emotion, that *every* queer and lesbian feel, in *every aspect* of their relationship, may well have *started out* in genuine love, as between two dear friends; BUT, once they stepped over the wee-wee/woo-woo line , it became *totally* perverted into LUST. Why? Because WEE-WEE WITH WOO-WOO IS THE ONLY WAY NATURE WORKS (don't forget WHERE DNA tells us babies come FROM). The Ph.D. might flail his/her arms in some girly way, or he/she might try to sub us down with a dykey frown, and say, "You are wrong. Don't ignore the numerous studies that have confirmed that these transgendered emotions are genuine affections, not mere lust." I would respond thus, "I agree that transgendered emotions are genuine affections; but don't *you* ignore, Doctor He/She, Ph.D., that Lust is *also* a genuine affection, and that God, Who wrote the DNA code, has definitively declared that ALL *such genuine affection* means "**burned in their lust** one toward another". And don't ignore that God also described these genuine affections as **vile affections**, and that vile means 'morally bad, wicked'." No "Love" to it...NONE at all... ONLY LUST—in every conceivable situation—ACCORDING TO GOD.

The Argument from Silence is generally considered a logical fallacy. But remember, The Bible is a COMPLETED Revelation—which contains Supersets of different stuff, *and therefore logically applies everything God ever said Scripturally to any and all that Subset Stuff*—THEREFORE, the Argument from Silence is valid...*when using Scripture!* The Bible is *not* an ordinary book. See?

> RULE #4—THE BIBLE IS THE STANDARD OF TRUTH.

> PSA 119:128 Therefore **I esteem all thy precepts concerning all things to be right**; and <u>I hate every false way</u>.

> ACT 17:11 These were more noble than those in Thessalonica, in that they received the word with all readiness of mind, and **searched the scriptures daily, whether those things were so**.

Remember—There are 1,500 fulfilled prophecies in The Bible, without a single miss. The simplest chance (50-50) of this happening by accident is 0.5^{1500}, or 1 chance in 3.51×10^{61}. The limits of mathematical meaningfulness in statistical calculations are $n \times 10^{\pm 50}$, so the odds of Chance fulfillment are *11 orders of magnitude less than meaningless*—simply put, ODDS OF $10^{\pm 51}$ OR MORE *DON'T MEAN SQUAT*. A professor of statistics will quickly point out that *improbability* of one choice *does not necessarily prove* any other choice (all of my stats profs, all the way up through graduate school, pounded that into our heads). But, when asked in *private*, "What if there are ONLY 2 POSSIBILITIES? Doesn't the *improbable* 'squatness' of one then *logically* imply the *probable* certainty of the other?" then, most of my stats profs declined to answer, but a couple just nodded quietly. You see, this is the heart of the process of Falsification, which is purportedly how scientists fumble forward to probable Truth. Unless of course, you are able to falsify evolution. *That*, they tell you, is unscientific. In other words, when discussing these 1,500 fulfilled prophecies, it's a virtual certainty that GOD DID IT.

Furthermore, there are 13,173 verses in The Bible. That gives us an average of one SCIENTIFICALLY CONFIRMED (by Archaeology) HISTORICALLY TRUE STATEMENT for every 17.3 verses...and that *validates* the credibility of The Bible. Furthermore, Such a Foreteller *must* be Infinite, Omniscient, and Omnipotent, to pull something like that off, over a 6,000 year period, *without a single miss*. And that, of course, constitutes the definition of God.

And God says of The Bible He claims to have inspired, word for word, "**All the words** of my mouth are in **righteousness**; there is **nothing froward or perverse in them**." (Prv 8:8). In other words, The Bible is the Standard of Truth. So...If you *ever* have A CHOICE BETWEEN *any* theory, claim, argument, philosophy, religion, vision, prophecy, or pontification of authority; AND *a clear cut Proof Text in The Bible, taken in its Primary Meanings, and supported with Par-*

allel Passages with due application of the Argument from Silence; THEN...*TAKE THE BIBLE EVERY TIME.*

Why? For these Proof Text reasons:

> Eph 4:13-14 Till we all come in **the unity of the faith**, and of **the knowledge of the Son of God**, unto a perfect man, unto the measure of the stature of the fulness of Christ: 14 That we henceforth be no more children, tossed to and fro, and carried about **with every wind of doctrine, by the sleight of men, and cunning craftiness, whereby they lie in wait to deceive**;

> 2 Cor 4:1-4 Therefore seeing we have this ministry, as we have received mercy, we faint not; 2 But have renounced **the hidden things of dishonesty, not walking in craftiness, nor handling the word of God deceitfully**; but by **manifestation of the truth** commending ourselves to every man's conscience in the sight of God. 3 But **if our gospel be hid**, it is hid to them that are lost: 4 In whom **the god of this world hath blinded the minds of them which believe not,** lest **the light of the glorious gospel of Christ,** who is the image of God, should shine unto them.

Supersets and Subsets. You see, all those DIFFERENT theories, claims, arguments, philosophies, religions, visions, prophecies, or pontifications of authorities *ultimately come from one single source*: THE GOD OF THIS WORLD. There are *only two* ultimate Sources of all ideas and opinions: The God of Heaven, and whom He calls The God of This World. Be careful Whom you pick—it's a one way Door...and it locks shut behind you.

As I have told you so many times before, The Bible is *not* an ordinary book.

RULE #5—SUBMIT TO THE WORD OF GOD
WHEN YOU UNDERSTAND IT.

> PSA 119:167 My soul **hath kept** thy testimonies; and I **love** them exceedingly. [Note the tenses!]

> ACT 17:11 These were more noble than those in Thessalonica, in that **they received the word with all readiness of mind**, and searched the scriptures daily, whether those things were so.

> 1SA 15:22 And Samuel said, Hath the LORD as great delight in burnt offerings and sacrifices, as in obeying the

voice of the LORD? **Behold, <u>to obey</u> is better than sacrifice, and to hearken than the fat of rams**.

ISA 28:9-13 **Whom shall he teach knowledge?** and whom shall he make to understand doctrine? them that are weaned from the milk, and drawn from the breasts. 10 For precept must be upon precept, precept upon precept; line upon line, line upon line; here a little, and there a little: 11 For with stammering lips and another tongue will he speak to this people. 12 To whom he said, This is the rest wherewith ye may cause the weary to rest; and this is the refreshing: **yet they would not hear.** 13 But the word of the LORD was unto them precept upon precept, precept upon precept; line upon line, line upon line; here a little, and there a little; **that they might go, and fall backward, and be broken, and snared, and taken.**

JAM 4:17 **Therefore to him that knoweth to do good, and doeth it not, <u>to him it is sin</u>.**

JAM 2:10 For whosoever shall keep the **whole** law, and **yet offend in <u>one</u> point**, he is **guilty of all**.

Of all the Principles and Rules of Bible Study, this last one is of the *most* practical importance. Yet of them all, it needs the least explanation—as stated, it is self-evident, and the Proof Texts show it so. In all of these passages, one common point underlies them all— Obeying what is Understood.

One of the saddest things any church is called upon to do, is withdrawing themselves from those who sin. It is not an option, nor a preference, it is a commandment.

> 1 COR 5:11 But now I have written unto you **not to keep company,** if <u>any man that is called a brother</u> be a fornicator, or covetous, or an idolater, or a railer, or a drunkard, or an extortioner; **with <u>such an one</u> no not to eat**.
>
> 2 THESS 3:6 Now **we <u>command</u> you**, brethren, in the name of our Lord Jesus Christ, that ye **withdraw yourselves from every brother that walketh disorderly, and not after the tradition which he received of us.**

There are five lists of exclusion offenses in the New Testament, plus a scattered few more (no need to get into all *that*, just stating the fact), which give us a total of a little more than fifty such sins of which Scripture says, "Let it not be once named among you." These are your normal, ordinary sins that all serious Bible Believers try to avoid. If you think of the Ten Commandments as the Superset (which it is), then these can be considered all the detailed Subsets (which they are). Some of these things are extremely serious, such as Murder, Extortion, Haters of God, Witchcraft, Covenantbreaking, and Idolatry. Most Bible Believers don't touch stuff like that with somebody else's ten foot pole. Then, there's all the rest of the stuff, like drunkenness, fornication, stealing, proud, railer and on and on. You know, all that stuff with which the troubles and trials of life tempt us so unmercifully. The only way most of us can make it through is by staying close to God in prayer, like a tiny Child holding on tightly to one of Daddy's fingers. That's why church discipline can be so difficult—sometimes, we have to vote to withdraw from someone for wading *way too deep* into something we might have a *little* of on the bottom of our own shoe, at the time.

I was the pastor of various congregations for 49 years, until God Who called me to that service impressed me strongly that I had finished my course. I still have a Teaching ministry, which is why I preach and write books, but I have laid down the shepherd's staff. Here is something that is weird. In all those 49 years, of all the people I have seen *necessarily* excluded from church, only about 15-20% were guilty of those normal, ordinary 50 some odd sins. Most excluded people in my personal experience, about 80-85% of them, were all...*every one of them*...guilty of *just one sin*—being a Stupid Butthead. Stupid means, "lacking intelligence or common sense; dazed and unable to think clearly." Butthead means, "a stupid or stubborn person." One of the reasons they are called buttheads is, it's so metaphorically *descriptive*. If a person's head were a butt, which has only one hole, that would be their mouth...and lo! behold what doth come forth—Crapola (which means "nonsense, rubbish"). Isn't that weird? Aren't Buttheads strange?

"Wait a minute," you say, "This is supposed to be a book on How to Study the Bible, and you are supposed to be teaching Rule #5 of Bible Study...what's all this talk about Buttheads?" My apologies, but that is *exactly* what I am trying to explain. Rule #5 *says*, Submit to the Word of God when you understand it. What that *means* is, "When you **UNDERSTAND** what The Words of God in The Word of God *say and mean*, with due regard for the 4 Principles and the other 4 Rules of Bible Study, **THEN DO IT**...*don't be a STUPID BUTTHEAD and willfully toss God's Word aside for your own CRAPOLA ideas.*

"Whoa!" you say, and stagger back. "You told me about Primary Meanings, and you insisted on Proof Texts. Can you prove all this Butthead stuff?" Sure I can. You don't think I would waste a whole page talking about it, if I couldn't prove it...do you? The words 'stupid', 'butthead', and 'crapola' do not appear in the King James Bible, but *synonyms*, which mean much the same thing, most assuredly do. But, we are not going that route. We are going to keep it simple as possible, but not any simpler, I'm going to give you a single Proof Text that *uses the definitions* of all three of these words; and therefore is *saying definitionally*, what I told you above, that Rule #5 *means*:

> 1 TIM 6:2b-5 ...These things teach and exhort. 3 **If any man teach otherwise, and consent not to wholesome words, even the words of our Lord Jesus Christ, and to the doctrine which is according to godliness;** 4 He is proud, **knowing nothing, but doting about questions and strifes of words**, whereof cometh envy, strife, railings, evil surmisings, 5 **Perverse disputings** of men of **corrupt minds**, and **destitute of the truth,** supposing that gain is godliness: from such withdraw thyself.

Is the definition of Stupid in there? Check the definition I gave above, then read carefully. How about **knowing nothing but doting about questions and strifes of words, destitute of the truth**? And here's the definition of Butthead: **Corrupt minds, consent not to wholesome words**. And of course, the definition of Crapola: **If any man teach otherwise, and consent not to...the words of our Lord Jesus Christ...the doctrine which is according to godliness, perverse disputings**. Finally, is THEN DO IT somewhere in there? How about, "from such withdraw thyself"? Can you say, "Stupid Butthead spouting Crapola?" *I knew you could!* See?

This is the single sin...exactly and precisely...which 80-85% of the people I have personally experienced being excluded from church, were guilty of WILLFULLY COMMITTING. That is about 4 out of 5 of them. Not all those *other* sins most of us struggle with constantly, and overcome only with God's grace. Oh, no. Just...this...one... Now, they *did* commit one or more of those other sins also. That's where they chose to dig their foxhole for the shootout. But, the *motive*, the *compelling reason* for the fight *at all*, was...They would not consent to the wholesome words of The Lord Jesus Christ, expressing the Doctrine of God in plain Bible verses, WORDS THAT ACTUALLY SAID IT. I cannot tell you how many times in 49 years...it seems times without number...in church fights (yes, that happens, usually because of these people), church courts (yes, churches at times hold actual courts), public debates (where at least it is expected), counseling sessions, living room discussions, Bible studies, evangelical meetings...every imaginable occasion...WHEN SHOWN A VERSE THAT SAYS IT, WITH THE WORDS DEFINED FROM A DICTIONARY, a Stupid Butthead would spout Crapola like, "That's just your opinion."

Example: I was doing evangelical work in Canada many years ago, teaching on a given doctrine, and cited a Proof Text and read key definitions from a dictionary. This Stupid Butthead interrupted the lesson by standing up and shouting, "That's just your opinion." I pointed out to him 1) I was reading a Bible verse, 2) I was reading definitions out of a dictionary, and 3) God had picked those words and quoted that verse to a writer who penned them down over 2000 ago. I explained that I had nothing to do with it, "It isn't *my* opinion. It's *God's* opinion. *You just do not believe God!*" The congregation actually began applauding. Butthead just stormed out.

What does all this mean? What is the *one point* for you to carry home? Simply this: RULE #5—SUBMIT TO THE WORD OF GOD WHEN YOU UNDERSTAND IT. It is just that simple. That one rule *alone* will solve about 85% of the problems in a Bible Believer's sojourn in this hell hole of a world. Why do it? Because The Bible is *not* an ordinary book—It literally is THE WORD OF GOD IN THE WORDS OF GOD.

Summary

We have summarized, proven, and illustrated the 4 Principles and the 5 Rules of How to Study The Bible. They comprises the basic toolkit of Hermeneutics. If you know these well, and almost nothing else, you'll do okay. If you have a Ph.D. in Hermeneutics from a seminary, and were *not* taught these, then you will run in circles. As I was shown, and as I have shown you, every single one of these Principles and Rules is *plainly taught* in The Word of God, in The Words of God. As Christ said, they are the Will of God which you *must do*, if you want to *learn* and *know* the Doctrine of God:

> John 7:15-17 And the Jews marvelled, saying, <u>How **knoweth** this man letters, having never **learned**</u>? 16 Jesus answered them, and said, My doctrine is not mine, but his that sent me. 17 <u>**If any man will do his will, he shall know of the doctrine,**</u> whether it be of God, or whether I speak of myself.

> Note—The Greek text puts it even stronger, being structured with an infinitive: **If any man will TO DO his will**. *This* is how one *learns* then *knows* the Doctrine of God... *not any other way*. Call it DIVINE HERMENEUTICS. It trumps *every other* kind.

EVERY HERESY THERE EVER HAS BEEN, IS NOW, OR EVER SHALL BE, INVOLVES A VIOLATION OF ONE, OR MORE, OF THESE BIBLICAL PRINCIPLES AND RULES!

*****

Chapter 3—Getting Down and Dirty (Examples)

Introduction—7 Core Doctrines
The Identity of God
Eternal Election
Faith OF God vs. Faith IN God
Regeneration before Faith
TULIP—The Plan of Salvation
Tent of Abraham, Tabernacle of Moses, Church of Christ
Amillennialism vs. all other -isms

Introduction—7 Core Doctrines

I have proven that God exists and have validated the credibility of The Bible (p. 55). I have definitively identified The Bible (Ch. 1). And, I have shown you God has told us How to Study The Bible (Ch. 2).

Now...let's do some of it.

There are 7 Core Doctrines that *define* The Religion of The Bible, listed above on the Chapter 3 title page. ANY AND ALL religion that does *not* embrace ALL of these 7 Core Doctrines is NEITHER *TRUE* NOR *BIBLICAL*, no matter how many Bible verses are scotch-taped to it.

It is also possible to invent a religion that has all 7 Core Doctrines, but then ADD A BUNCH OF CRAPOLA to it, thus making it neither neither True nor Biblical, EVEN THOUGH IT HAS ALL 7 CORE DOCTRINES.

Whoa! Stagger back! How is *that* possible? By VIOLATING one, or more, of the 4 Principles and 5 Rules of Bible Study. Wow! How do you do that? One quick example. You can do like the Infallible Roman Pope did: Start with The Bible; then *add* the apocryphal books to it; then *change* thousands of Bible verses necessary to scotch-tape it all together; and finally *leave out* or *add in* hundreds of verses, as you wish...you know, as Satan taught Eve to do, in the Garden of Eden (p. 34). See?

You *must* learn to do 2 things: 1) Think, and 2) Use *only* The Bible. "How?", you may ask. First, Get a Brain Crutch (pp. 10-11). Then, hobble along *only* through a King James Bible (in English), with the appropriate Hebrew and Greek texts. USE *NOTHING ELSE*.

Now, hobbling on a Brain Crutch and using *only* a King James Bible, let's apply what we have learned about How to Study The Bible to *define* and *prove* each of these 7 Core Doctrines.

The Identity of God

> Deut 6:4-5 **Hear** (*Shama* H8085), **O Israel: The LORD our God is one LORD**: 5 And thou shalt love the LORD thy God with all thine heart, and with all thy soul, and with all thy might.

As Jesus Christ said (Mark 12:28-30), this is "The first of all the commandments." As we saw in detail (pp. 43-45), this passage identifies the Creator God as *Yehovah Elohim*, "LORD God" in the King James Bible, which literally means, "The-eternally-Self-existent-One,

The-at-least-three-Mighty-Ones". "One LORD" in Hebrew is *echad Yehovah*, which literally means in English, "The-eternally-Self-existent-One United-into-One" (Heb reads right to left). Thus we learned that the LORD God—*Yehovah Elohim*—is a Trinity...three distinct *Personalities* cohering in one single undivided divine *Nature*...exactly as the Apostle John, writing by inspiration declared in his first letter:

> 1 John 5:7 For **there are three** that bear record in heaven, **the Father, the Word, and the Holy Ghost**: and **these three are one**.

These are the *exact* Words that God quoted unto Moses and John, who wrote them down *exactly*, and then God preserved them in copying and translating (in *some* lines of manuscripts) so that *none* of His Words did fall to the ground. Thus we have them as *exactly* in the King James Bible today, as they were given in the *original* Hebrew and Greek thousands of years ago. God is an *Infinite* Being, explaining His Divine Nature, in His chosen Words, to *finite* human beings...Three *are* One, and One *is* Three...the Trinity (Three in One, *Elohim*) is a Unicity (absolute Oneness, *Yehovah*). Our finite minds may not *fully* understand HOW such can be, but we *can* understand *without excuse* THAT is what God said. Some believe it, and to that degree show evidence of their salvation; some refuse to believe it, and to that degree show evidence of their damnation. That's just the way it is.

> Rom 3:3-4 For **what if some did not believe? shall their unbelief make the faith of God without effect? 4 God forbid: yea, let God be true, but every man a liar**; as it is written, That thou mightest be justified in thy sayings, and mightest overcome when thou art judged.

There's more. Consider the following passage:

> Exo 3:14-15 And God said unto Moses, **I AM THAT I AM**: and he said, Thus shalt thou say unto the children of Israel, **I AM** hath sent me unto you.
> 15 **And God said moreover unto Moses**, Thus shalt thou say unto the children of Israel, The **LORD God** of your fathers, the God of Abraham, the God of Isaac, and the God of Jacob, hath sent me unto you: **this is my name for ever, and this is my memorial unto all generations**.

Another Name that God declares for Himself is I AM THAT I AM. In Hebrew, this Name is *Ehyeh Asher Ehyeh* (*Ehyeh* is a Qal-form verb, ~ present tense in Eng.; *Asher* is a pronoun), which transliterated grammatically into English is, "I-continuously-AM THAT-Being

I-continuously-AM." This Name emphasizes God's absolute, eternal, self-existence.

The two Names, LORD (*Yehovah*) and I AM THAT I AM, taken together, emphasize the Absolute Eternal Oneness of God—THERE IS *ONLY ONE*.

> Isa 44:6,8b Thus saith the LORD the King of Israel, and his redeemer the LORD of hosts; **I am the first, and I am the last; and <u>beside me there is no God</u>**.…8b <u>**Is there a God beside me? yea, there is no God; I know not any.**</u>
>
> Isa 45:5-6 **I am the LORD, and <u>there is none else, there is no God beside me</u>**: I girded thee, though thou hast not known me: 6 That they may know from the rising of the sun, and from the west, that **<u>there is none beside me.</u> I am the LORD,<u> and there is none else</u>**.
>
> Isa 45:21b-22 <u>**There is no God else beside me**</u>; **a just God and a Saviour; <u>there is none beside me.</u>** 22 Look unto me, and be ye saved, all the ends of the earth: for **<u>I am God, and there is none else</u>**.

One more thing. God tells us the short form of I AM THAT I AM is simply I AM (Heb, *Ehyeh*). Now, check *this* out:

> John 8:56-59 [Jesus speaking] **<u>Your father Abraham rejoiced to see my day: and he saw it, and was glad.</u>** 57 Then said the Jews unto him, Thou art not yet fifty years old, and hast thou seen Abraham?
> 58 Jesus said unto them, **Verily, verily, I say unto you, Before Abraham was, I AM.** 59 Then took they up stones to cast at him: but Jesus hid himself, and went out of the temple, going through the midst of them, and so passed by.

Remember, Jesus has *two natures*: **1** His human nature, born of a Virgin, thus just like ours (except without sin); and **2** His divine Nature, The Word, the Second Person of the Trinity, The LORD (*Yehovah*), Who conjoined Himself to the zygote (the single fertilized cell) at the Miraculous Conception. Taking John 8:56-59 together with Exo 3:14-15, we come to the *undeniable conclusion* that THE DIVINE NATURE OF THE LORD JESUS CHRIST—I AM, *YEHOVAH*—WAS THE GOD OF ABRAHAM.

There is a **Fatal Problem for Muslims**. The Holy Koran tells Muslims to "read The Book," which means The Bible. The Book, The Bible, tells us that The Lord Jesus Christ was The God of Abraham. Here is the Fatal Problem. The Holy Koran teaches that Jesus was a

Prophet of God, but denies that He was God. Jesus the Prophet said in The Book that He was I AM, the God of Abraham. Thus, the Holy Koran is False. *It gets worse.* If the Holy Koran is True, and Jesus is not I AM, the God of Abraham, then Jesus is *not* a Prophet of God, as the Holy Koran says, but only a *Liar*; thus, the Holy Koran is False. Observe, there are *only two possibilities*; and no matter which one you pick, LOGICALLY THE HOLY KORAN PROVES FALSE. This, you see is a Fatal Problem for Muslims. Before anybody says anything, Remember that The Bible (The Book) has 1500 fulfilled prophecies, without a single miss; but the Holy Koran *does not have even a single Bible-type prophecy*...NOT EVEN ONE. Everything that I have shown you in this paragraph is undeniable fact. True Religion is based upon undeniable fact, False Religion *denies* undeniable fact. One more undeniable fact: I have helped convert Muslims into baptized Christians by showing them these undeniable facts.

There is a **Fatal Problem for** *ALL* **non-Christian religions,** *especially Occult Babylonian Talmudism* (which is NOT Mosaism, but has *claimed* to be 'Judaism' since ~150 AD)—THE DIVINE NATURE OF JESUS CHRIST, THE GOD OF ABRAHAM, IS **THE ONLY GOD THAT EXISTS**. *Ain Soph*, the god of Kabbalah, is only Crapola.

For all people everywhere, who believe and love The Word of The God of Abraham in the Words of The God of Abraham,

> Jer 9:23-24 **Thus saith the LORD**, Let not the wise man glory in his wisdom, neither let the mighty man glory in his might, let not the rich man glory in his riches:
> 24 But **let him that glorieth glory in this, that <u>he understandeth and knoweth me, that I am the LORD</u>** which exercise lovingkindness, judgment, and righteousness, in the earth: **for <u>*in these things I delight*</u>, saith the LORD.**

As the old hymn sings,

> Praise God from Whom all blessings flow;
> Praise Him all creatures here below;
> Praise Him above ye Heavenly Host;
> Praise Father, Son, and Holy Ghost.
> Amen.
> —The Doxology

Eternal Election

> Eph 1:3-6 Blessed be the God and Father of our Lord Jesus Christ, who hath blessed us with all spiritual blessings

> in heavenly places in Christ: 4 **According as he hath chosen us in him before the foundation of the world**, that we should be holy and without blame before him in love: 5 Having predestinated us **unto the adoption of children** by Jesus Christ to himself, according to the good pleasure of his will, 6 To the praise of the glory of his grace, wherein **he hath made us accepted in the beloved. 7 In whom we have redemption through his blood, the forgiveness of sins**, according to the riches of his grace;

Remember, this is a Proof Text. I even used it as an example back on p. #35. A Proof Text *says* it. Look carefully again at what this text *says*. Now, let me tell you what it *means*: *Every one* whose sins are forgiven in Christ, *every one* who is redeemed by the blood of Christ, *every one* who is accepted in Christ, *every one* who is adopted a Child of God by Christ...*every one, without a single exception*...WAS CHOSEN IN CHRIST, *BY* GOD THE FATHER, *BEFORE* THE FOUNDATION OF THE WORLD. See? It *means* what it *says*.

Now, let me tell you what it *does not* mean: It *does not* mean that you have to free will choose Jesus Christ as your Saviour, open the door of your heart, and let Him come in, so He can *then* choose you *before the foundation of the world*. Think about that—it's butt-dumb stupid. That's one of the reasons government schools removed the Brain Crutch (p. 10-11) over 50 years ago, so people would slog around in stupid word sludge like that, instead of reading their Bibles and demanding the government obey Scripture, as the Founding Fathers taught us over 200 years ago. The other reason is more political—so American voters would vote in Socialism, and loose the last of their freedoms on the way to a one-world police state. They did that in 2012, when they re-elected Obama...*how's that working out?*

When Eternal Salvation is concerned, *no saved person EVER chooses God...God chooses EVERY saved person...BEFORE the foundation of the world.*

> John 15:16 (Christ speaking) **Ye have not chosen me, but I have chosen you**, and ordained you, that ye should go and bring forth fruit, and that your fruit should remain: that whatsoever ye shall ask of the Father in my name, he may give it you.

Just *when* do you think Jesus Christ did that choosing? Clue: Before the foundation of the _____ (fill in the blank). How do I know this? I read the notes on the cheat sheet...here they are:

> Rev 13:8 And all that dwell upon the earth shall worship him (the Beast), **whose names are not written in the book**

of life of the Lamb slain <u>from the foundation of the world</u>.

Rev 17:8 The beast that thou sawest was, and is not; and shall ascend out of the bottomless pit, and go into perdition: and they that dwell on the earth shall wonder, whose names were not **written in the book of life <u>from the foundation of the world</u>**, when they behold the beast that was, and is not, and yet is.

Rev 20:11- And I saw a great white throne, and him that sat on it, from whose face the earth and the heaven fled away; and there was found no place for them. 12 And I saw the dead, small and great, stand before God; and the books were opened: and **another book was opened, which is <u>the book of life</u>**: and the dead were judged out of those things which were written in the books, <u>according to their works</u>....15 **And whosoever was not found written in <u>the book of life</u> was cast into the lake of fire.**

You see, WORKS is what unregenerate people *love* to do, when they think God *can't*. GRACE is what regenerate people *hope God did*, when they *know they couldn't*. Finally, let's draw SOME CONCLUSIONS.

1. On Judgement Day, Everybody who is depending upon their free will and works goes to Hell. Bad works—like slicing peoples' throats and eating chunks of them raw, like some Islamic Fundamentalists on YouTube; or murdering babies and selling their body parts, like on the Planned Parenthood films, which the government was subsidizing—doing bad stuff like that, that's understandable. But, some of these folk also did what everybody thought were Good works—like *accepting* Jesus into their hearts and *letting* Him save them (can you find a single verse *that says that* in a King James Bible? Remember Bible Study Rule #3); or putting a dollar in the collection plate on Sunday, out of a $1200 paycheck (check out Lk 21:1-2); or dropping a *whole* quarter in a beggar's tin cup (Lk 16:19-31). Neither free will choices nor any works, good or bad...*whatsoever*...are sufficient for eternal salvation—*everyone* depending upon their works goes to Hell...*not a single exception.*

2. On Judgement Day, Everybody written in The Lamb's Book of Life goes to Heaven. *Not one* of their free will acts is considered, *not one* of their good works plays any part—*nothing* that they thought, decided, or did counts for squat. The *only* thing that matters is: Their Name, written in The Book of Life...*period.*

3. When the world was founded, during Creation Week, *all* of those names *were already written* in The Lamb's Book of Life. That means those names were written in the Book of Life *before* the foundation of the world, and that was *precisely when* God the Father *chose them* in The Lord Jesus Christ.

Now, let's use a Brain Crutch (pp. 10-11), to grammatically nail this stuff to the bedrock. Consider the phrase, "He hath chosen us in Him," In Eph 1:4 above. Basic Grammar using the 8 Parts of Speech (specifically Nouns, Pronouns, and antecedents) declares *undeniably* that God the Father chose us in The Lord Jesus Christ—*none of us* chose Him (we weren't even there), *exactly* as the parallel passage John 15:16 states. The *underlying* Greek text (*not* one of those Roman Catholic manuscripts) says it *exactly* the same.

Now, the word "chose" translates the Greek word *G1586 eklegomai*. Here is what they both *mean*:

choose. Pick out or select (someone or something) as being the best or most appropriate of two or more alternatives. [Oxford American]

eklegomai. To *select*. [Strong's Hebrew Lexicon]

Next, let's define the synonym (a word that means the same, or nearly the same, as another) that names the doctrine we are studying:

elect. Verb. Christian Theology (of God) choose (someone) in preference to others for salvation.
Adjective. Christian Theology chosen by God for salvation. [Oxford American]

Then, observe that "chosen...before the foundation of the world" means the same as "Eternal Election", the doctrine we are studying. Finally, remember what the Elect are chosen *for*? The Remission of Sins, through Christ's blood; Redemption from Sins, through Christ's blood; thus made Accepted in Christ and Adopted as Children by Christ. That, in a nutshell, is the Doctrine of Eternal Election. Of course, there is a great deal more, that fleshes out *each of those specific points*, but this is not a book on Bible Doctrine, just a book on How to Study The Bible.

But...I want to show you one more thing: What God Planned to do, and How Satan tried to stop it. It makes all of this Election Stuff as clear as a bell.

Here is what God Planned to do:

> Gen 1:26-28a **And God said, Let us make man in our image, after our likeness:** and let them have dominion... 27 So God created man in his own image, in the image of God created he him; male and female created he them. 28 And God blessed them, and God said unto them, Be fruitful, and multiply, and replenish the earth, and subdue it...
>
> Gen 2:16 And the LORD God commanded the man, saying, Of every tree of the garden thou mayest freely eat: 17 **But of the tree of the knowledge of good and evil, thou shalt not eat of it: for in the day that thou eatest thereof thou shalt surely die.**
>
> Note—Adam and Eve were given Immortal Life (never age or die *from anything within themselves*), and given dominion over the earth, to subdue it ("overcome, quieten, or bring under control"—they were *not* tree-huggers). God planned for them *to have children*. With nobody dying, there would have been *a lot* of them. There was *one way* to die in Paradise, but God gave them *sufficient warning*.

Here is how Satan tried to stop it:

> Bottom line. Satan deceived Eve into eating, because he knew Adam's love for her was his *one* weakness—as Adam's actions show, he loved Eve *more* than he loved God. They both ate, and died (Gen 3:1-11), and Jesus says Satan was "a murderer from the beginning" and the Father of the Lie (John 8:44). *Then...* this happened...pay very close attention what Scripture *says*:
>
> Gen 3:14-16a And **the LORD God said unto the serpent**, Because thou hast done this, thou art cursed above all cattle, and above every beast of the field; upon thy belly shalt thou go, and dust shalt thou eat all the days of thy life: 15 And **I will put enmity between thee and the woman, and between <u>thy seed</u> and <u>her seed</u>; it shall bruise thy head, and thou shalt bruise his heel.**
>
> 16 <u>Unto the woman he said</u>, **I will greatly multiply** thy sorrow and **thy conception**;

Now consider what this *means*. First, God said He was going to "greatly multiply" Eve's conception. In other words, she was going to have *a lot more children* than were first intended—there were going to be A LOT OF EXTRA PEOPLE...*because* of that Fall. Second, notice that all the children God originally planned for are called HER SEED (the One that would bruise the Serpent's head of course was Christ... *but there were others*). Third, notice that *God calls ALL THE EXTRA PEOPLE SATAN'S SEED*. Why? Because Satan...*and Satan alone...*

bears *paternal responsibility* for their existence. God is paternally responsible *only* for the existence of Adam and Eve and all of their children.

Here is what makes all of this Election Stuff as clear as a bell. SATAN'S SEED are *all the Extra People*, who are judged out of the books according to their works on Judgement Day, and are all sent to Hell... and now you *know* Why. Who are Those Written in The Lamb's Book of Life? Adam and Eve and all their children—*Who would have been born anyway, had there been no Fall.* Now, you *understand* Why. The ELECT (who *all* go to Heaven) are all of the people that would have been born anyway had there been no sin. The NON-ELECT (who *all* go to Hell) are all of the Extra People, who were born *only because Satan murdered Adam and Eve, the way he did.* Clear as a bell. See?

One final comment. When, *exactly*, did God make the Choice of Election...in Eternity or in Time? This is part of what is called, The Order of God's Decrees. The answer is...Both, sorta. Whoa! Stagger back. "How could that be?" you ask. Good question. The answer involves both Plan and Action.

> Act 15:18 Known unto God are **all** his works **from** the beginning of the world.

The reason God knows everything He is going to do *from* the beginning of the world, is that He *Planned* it all in Eternity, *before* He began the world. Now, let me show you how God *Acted out* His Eternal Election *Plan*, from the beginning of the world:

> Rom 9:20-24 Nay but, O man, who art thou that repliest against God? Shall the thing formed say to him that formed it, Why hast thou made me thus? 21 **Hath not the potter power over the clay, of <u>the same lump</u>** [G5445 *phurama*] **to make one vessel unto honour, and another unto dishonour?**
>
> 22 What if God, willing to show his wrath, and to make his power known, endured with much longsuffering the **vessels of wrath fitted to destruction**: 23 And that he might make known the riches of his glory on the **vessels of mercy, which <u>he</u> had afore prepared unto glory**, 24 Even us, whom he hath called, not of the Jews only, but also of the Gentiles?

> **lump**. A compact mass of a substance, especially one without a definite or regular shape. [Oxford American]
>
> ***phurama***. (to *mix* a liquid with a solid...through the idea of swelling in bulk), mean to *knead*; a *mass* of dough. [Strong's Hebrew Lexicon]

Like a potter with clay, God took a lump to shape. A lump, like a mass of dough, *has no shape*. But, Adam and Eve were *created* in the Image of God (Gen 1:26-27). What happened to that 'shape'? They sinned, and fell, *and lost that image*. Then, *out of that shapeless lump of fallen humanity*, God chose (election) to "prepare...vessels of mercy...unto glory"—all the Children He *Planned* to have in Eternity, He now *Acted* to save in Time. The rest of the lump, He did not choose (non-election), but as v22 says, left for Satan to "fit to destruction." With their respective lumps, both God and Satan have done a *superb* job. God *Planned* it all in Eternity, then God *Acted* it out in Time.

In studying the Order of God's decrees...Creation, Permit the Fall, Election of Saved and Non-election of Damned...there are two popular Orders in which folks believe God did these things:

Sublapsarian (*after* the Fall)—Create, Fall, Elect.
Supralapsarian (*before* the Fall)—Elect, Create, Fall.

In Sublapsarianism, God elects *after* the Fall, to restore His Own Children, leaving the Extra People right where Satan put them. In Supralapsarianism, God does *both* His Planning and Acting in Eternity, choosing to make some Saved People (elect) *and to make some Damned People* (non-elect)—logically, this would make God responsible for the Damned. Some folks believe that Rom 9:20-24 *means* what it *says*, so they are Sublapsarians. Other folks, who believe John Calvin, believe that Rom 9:20-24 *means* what John Calvin *says*, so are Supralapsarians. What do I believe? I believe Bible Study Rule #5. The most important question is, What do *you* believe?

Faith *OF* God vs. Faith *IN* God

> 2 Cor 1:9-10 But we had the sentence of death in ourselves, that we should not trust in ourselves, but in God which raiseth the dead: 10 **Who <u>delivered</u> us from so great a death, and <u>doth deliver</u>: in whom we trust that he <u>will yet deliver</u> us;**

"Whoa! Wait a minute," you say; "Where's Faith in that passage?" It's not in there, I answer. "Then what's the point?" you ask. Good question. You see, the *effects*, the *results*, of God's Faith and Our Faith *are* right there...in plain sight. See? "No, I don't," you say. Sorry, let me explain.

> **deliver**. (deliver someone/something from) save, rescue, or set free from. [Oxford American]

There are 3 Salvations in this text. I'll just point them out, and we can comment on them later, if need be.

> "Who delivered us from so great a death"—Past tense: This is <u>Eternal Salvation</u>, delivering us from the great death of humanity, the *Penalty* of Sin, which occurred from the Fall in the Garden of Eden; it results in *Sonship of the saved.*
>
> "And doth deliver"—Present tense: This is <u>Time Salvation</u>, which happens here in this time world, when people whom God has *first* eternally saved by His grace, are *later* exposed to the Call of the Gospel, hear and obey, and become baptized Christians, and are thus *saved to Fellowship* with God, from the *Practice* of Sin (yes, there is Time Damnation for eternally saved people, who *disobey* the Gospel Call, but we'll talk about that later...No, it isn't fun, not at all).
>
> "He will yet deliver us"—Future tense: This the Resurrection of the Body, from death in the grave, saving the Elect from the *Presence* of Sin (since everybody will experience some form of this, it need not concern us further).

That leaves two salvations to consider. Let's summarize at this point by saying: Faith OF God *produces* Eternal Salvation to *Sonship* and Resurrection of the Body, Faith IN God *enables* Time Salvation to *Fellowship* for the Sons.

Now...we get down to it.

Faith OF God is what God does. Faith IN God is what eternally saved Children of God do. "Wait a minute," you say, "How do eternally saved Children of God, well, get eternally saved?" By Faith OF God...what God does...and their Faith IN God, what they do, has *nothing* to do with it. See? Oh, then let me explain.

Remember Eternal Election, how God chose His people before the foundation of the world? And how God wrote their names in the Lamb's Book of Life (identifying the Ones for whom the Lamb would die, on that Cross)? And how Jesus Christ chose us and we didn't choose Him? Well, *that* is how the eternally saved Children get eternally saved. It is *part* of the Faith OF God, which we are going to talk about in a moment. Our Faith IN God we will discuss next, in the Doctrine of Regeneration before Faith, so we'll mostly leave that until then.

Finally...the Faith OF God. For what is coming next, we are going to need that Brain Crutch again. There are those who insist that some will need a wheel chair, or even a gurney...but we won't go there. The Brain Crutch will be sufficient. Just remember what the Apostle Peter said,

> 2Pe 3:15b-18 ...Our beloved brother Paul also according to the wisdom given unto him hath written unto you; 16 As also **in all his epistles, speaking in them of these things; in which are some things hard to be understood,** which they that are unlearned and unstable wrest, as they do also the other scriptures, unto their own destruction. 17 Ye therefore, beloved, seeing ye know these things before, beware lest ye also, being led away with the error of the wicked, fall from your own stedfastness. 18 But grow in grace, and in the knowledge of our Lord and Saviour Jesus Christ. To him be glory both now and for ever. Amen.

You see, there are two things we have to deal with: Honest Mistake but with *serious* unintended consequences, and Devious Lie which brings *destruction*. The Honest Mistake comes when learning those things "hard to be understood". The Faith OF God is one of them. The Devious Lie comes from wicked and unstable men who never learned, but who decided to lie about it, and twist the Scriptures to their own destruction...and sadly, to the destruction of others. How did they twist Scripture? By intentionally violating one or more of the 4 Principles and 5 Rules of Bible Study, as I have shown you Satan did to Eve in the Garden of Eden.

The Lie was called Gnosticism (from Gk. *gnosis,* knowledge), a pagan system of salvation contemporary with early Christianity, but originating in antiquity (we can trace it back to early Sumeria with surviving clay tablets). It taught that eternal salvation from this material world necessarily came thru esoteric knowledge (*gnosis*) taught by secret societies, which one must learn, believe, and follow. Early Christian heretics adopted this paganism as follows: The secret *gnosis* was interpreted as a hidden message in the Gospel. If one would learn that gospel message, believe it, and be initiated thru the rite of baptism, then they would be eternally saved from their sins and from this material world. By late in the first century and early in the second, as this heresy grew in popularity, it developed into Neo-gnosticism (i.e., new gnosticism) and was substituted *openly* in place of early Christian doctrine. It was nothing more than Free Will Doctrine for eternal salvation: Hear the Gospel, believe it and let God save you, and be baptized, and you will receive eternal salvation. The churches historically recognizable as proto-catholic (those which would later be instrumental in forming the Catholic Church) swooped it up with enthusiasm. By 325 AD, when the pagan Roman emperor Constantine proclaimed his substitute Roman Catholic Church,

Neo-gnosticism (Free Will Doctrine for eternal salvation) was the hub of the catholic wheel. Just remember 3 things: 1) The Church that Jesus Christ founded was over 292 years old by 325 AD; 2) Jesus Christ was baptized by John, whom Jesus identified four times as "The Baptist"; and 3) When a Baptist preacher baptizes some one, they do *not* come out of the water as a Methepiscoterianatholicampbellitormon—Jesus Christ, a Baptist, founded a Baptist church. See?

The new Roman Catholic Church rapidly 'discovered' a whole bunch of manuscripts that nobody had seen before. Remember? We talked about that in Chapter 1…there's a neat review table on p.17 you might want to glance over. Lots of new verses were added in, lots of old verses were left out, thousands of verses were changed to read… *differently*…and a bunch of new books were added. These Roman Catholic manuscripts have become the basis for all the new modern revised bibles. One of the things the new modern revised bibles have *changed* is verses that teach Faith OF God, particularly the ones that read in a King James Bible (and the Gk. *Textus Receptus*) as "Faith OF Christ" (remember, the divine nature of Christ *is* God). That is why the new modern revised bibles *SUCK*—demons *suck* hellfire from ancient Roman Catholic manuscripts, *puke* it into the minds of modern translators (it leaves splatter stains called 'copyrights'), and thence it *drivels* into careless peoples' souls:

> 1 Tim 4:1 Now the Spirit speaketh expressly, that **in the latter times** some shall depart from **the faith**, giving heed to seducing spirits, and doctrines of devils;

In *some* of the Proof Text verses that deal with Faith OF God, and in *nearly all* of the Proof Text verses that deal with Faith OF Christ (remember, the divine nature of Christ *is* God), the new modern revised bible translators do what Satan taught Eve to do with the Word of God—they change it, add to it, deny it, or just revise it around to read the way they want it to. *How did that work out for Adam and Eve?*

That is why you need that Brain Crutch. The new modern bible translators play GRAMMAR GAMES with some Faith OF God Proof Texts, and with nearly all Faith OF Christ Proof Texts. They explain away the genitive case, so that Faith OF Christ really means Faith IN Christ (like Satan said "*surely* die" really means "*not* surely die"). They sometimes ignore the subjunctive mood, or worse, they will interpret a conditional subjunctive to mean a hypothetical subjunctive, which turns everything around backwards, making Faith OF Christ mean Faith IN Christ. Let's use that gorilla finger again. Do you *know* what the genitive case is, and what it means in a sentence? Do you *know* what the subjunctive mood is? Do you *know* the two most frequently used forms of subjunctive mood? Do you *know* what *each* form means, when used in a sentence? Can you *diagram* those sentences on paper, *correctly*, and show *what* goes *where* and *why*? If your answer is "No" to *any* of these questions, then I ask you, "How do you KNOW that you will NOT surely die, *if you EAT that new revised bible version CRAP?* This is why you need that Brain Crutch.

Grab the Brain Crutch tightly, and first hobble *This Way* through the Genitive Case. First, the genitive case Primary Meaning for Nouns and Pronouns is "source or origin". 'Genitive' comes from the Latin *genitivus* meaning "production or origin", itself from a word meaning "beget or generation" (see grammar book or dictionary). As we shall see, when The Bible *says* Faith OF God and Faith OF Christ ('of' indicating the genitive, as I learned *in the fifth grade*...and as kids in most *private* schools and home schools *still* learn), It *means* 'the faith that *originates* in God or Christ'. Let's read some places where It *says* it:

> Psa 40:10 I have not hid thy righteousness within my heart; **I have declared thy faithfulness and thy salvation**: I have not concealed thy lovingkindness and thy truth from the great congregation.
>
> Psa 92:1-2 It is a good thing to give thanks unto the LORD, and to **sing praises unto thy name, O most High: 2 To show forth** thy lovingkindness in the morning, and **thy faithfulness every night,**
>
> Rom 3:3 For what if some did not believe? **shall their unbelief make the faith of God without effect?**
>
> 2 Thss 3:3 But **the Lord is faithful**, who shall stablish you, and keep you from evil.
>
> 2 Tim 2:13 **If we believe not, yet he abideth faithful**: he cannot deny himself.

Observe—The last three passages *eliminate* the Free Will of man in Eternal Salvation (which establishes Sonship). Subsequently however, the Freed Will of the eternally saved person is *essential* in obtaining Time Salvation (which establishes Fellowship). More about this in following sections.

We need to learn more about Faith, don't we? Here is God's definition, in His Words, right out of His Word,

> Heb 11:1 Now **faith** is the substance of things hoped for, the evidence of things not seen.
>
> English = 1 complete trust or confidence in someone or something. 2 strong belief in God or in the doctrines of a religion, based on spiritual apprehension rather than proof. [Oxford American]

> Greek *pistis* G4102 = persuasion, credence, conviction. [Strong's Gk. Lexicon] Note—the different forms of this Gk. word imply PERSUASION RESULTING FROM ARGUMENT AND/OR EVIDENCE, the *exact opposite* of popular religion's "just believe" twaddle.
>
> Biblical Faith—Because God cannot lie (Tit 1:2) and because He is the Author and Finisher of our Faith (Heb 12:2), our faith may be counted both *as if* the tangible *substance* of what we believe and also as the *evidence* of it.

From Heb 11:1 we learn that there are *two* kinds of Faith:

> 1. Faith in the Known (which rests upon Evidence).
> 2. Faith in the Unknown (which rests upon Testimony).
>
> **John 14:11 Believe me that I am in the Father, and the Father in me** [type 2-Testimony]: **or else believe me for the very works' sake** [type 1-Evidence].

The Problem—In matters of Theology, most people concentrate upon *their* Faith, which simply believes the Testimony of God—Type 2, Faith in the Unknown. They forget that God, Who knows all things, most certainly *believes* in what He knows (just as people believe in what they know). Therefore, God has Faith and Faithfulness, because He *knows* that He is omnipotent and that nothing exists able to prevent His Purposes. Therefore, the Faith OF God and the Faith OF Christ is Type 1—Faith in the Known.

> **Dan 4:35** And all the inhabitants of the earth are reputed as nothing: and he doeth according to his will in the army of heaven, and among the inhabitants of the earth: and **none can stay his hand, or say unto him, What doest thou?**
>
> **Isa 46:9-11** Remember the former things of old: for **I am God, and there is none else; I am God, and there is none like me**, 10 Declaring the end from the beginning, and from ancient times the things that are not yet done, saying, **My counsel shall stand, and I will do all my pleasure**: 11 Calling a ravenous bird from the east, the man that executeth my counsel from a far country: **yea, I have spoken it, I will also bring it to pass; I have purposed it, I will also do it.**

Now, grab the Brain Crutch again, and next hobble *This Way* through the Subjunctive Mood. The Primary Meaning of Subjunctive Mood with Verbs and Adverbs is "relating to or denoting a mood of verbs expressing what is imagined or wished or possible" [Oxford American]. Two of the most frequent uses of the Subjunctive Mood are Conditional (*do* this *for* that) and Hypothetical (*if* this *then* that). Here is an example of each.

> Conditional: READ a grammar book, that you MIGHT understand The Word of God.
> Hypothetical: IF you don't learn grammar, THEN I'm gonna keep slapping you upside the head, like Gibbs does Tony.

As Einstein recommended, Let's keep this as simple as possible, but not any simpler. First, here it is as simple as possible. Four passages using the Conditional Subjunctive, to show that some action is done *to manifest* some *previous condition* that *makes that action possible*—

> Rom 3:26 "might be...the justifier of him which believeth in Jesus"
> Phlp 3:8-9 "may win Christ...not having mine own righteousness"
> Gal 2:16 "we have believed...that we might be justified,"
> Gal 3:22 "that the promise...might be given to them that believe"

Second, here comes the hard part—we have got to make it "not any simpler". We are going back through all four passages one by one, this time *in full*, analyze them grammatically using the Genitive Case and Subjunctive Mood, to make sure we know what they *say*, so we can *then* understand for sure what they *mean*.

> ★ Rom 3:21-26 But now **the righteousness of God without the law is manifested**, being witnessed by the law and the prophets; 22 **Even THE RIGHTEOUSNESS OF GOD WHICH IS BY FAITH OF JESUS CHRIST** unto all and upon all them that **believe**: for there is no difference: 23 For all have sinned, and come short of the glory of God; 24 Being justified freely by his grace through the redemption that is in Christ Jesus: 25 **Whom God hath set forth to be a propitiation through faith in his blood**, to declare his righteousness for the remission of sins that are past, through the forbearance of God; 26 To declare, I say, at this time his righteousness: that he **might** be just, and the justifier of him which **believeth** in Jesus.

> 1. Vs 21, without the law manifested—The Law does not bring the Righteousness of God, but rather *testifies* to and *manifests* it.
> 2. Vs 22, the Righteousness of God comes by Faith OF Jesus Christ—by Him keeping the terms of the Eternal Covenant upon the cross.

a. Vss 22-24,26; Human faith is not conditional here—human faith *manifests* that *both* God's *and* Christ's covenant faith has *already* justified them.
   b. OF God, OF Jesus Christ—genitive case, possessive; primary meaning is source or origin...*They* did it.
   c. Key Point—the Righteousness of God is established by the Covenant Faith OF Jesus Christ, *not* the free will faith of the sinner.
   d. Vs 25, the Mutual Faith OF the Godhead in Eternal Salvation—The Father saved elect people all along, because He *believed* Christ would be faithful to die on the cross as agreed; Christ was faithful to die on the cross, because He *believed* The Father would accept His Sacrifice as full payment for the Elect (They Both *believed* it because They Both *knew* it—Dan 4:35; Isa 46:9-11; see both passages again, above).
3. It is God's Mutual Covenant Faith that saves the Elect eternally. Their faith, obtaining Time Salvation, merely manifests that God has *already* eternally saved them. Indeed, without *first* being eternally saved, *they* COULD NOT and WOULD NOT *believe* AT ALL.

1 Jn 5:1a Whosoever **believeth** [present tense] that Jesus is the Christ **is born** [present perfect tense] of God...

Note—The present perfect tense (getting born) takes place *before* the present tense (believing), in all cases without exception (whosoever).

★ Phlp 3:8-9 Yea doubtless, and I count all things but loss for the excellency of the knowledge of Christ Jesus my Lord: for whom I have suffered the loss of all things, and do count them but dung, that I **may** win Christ, 9 And be found in him, **not having mine own righteousness**, which is of the law, **but that which is THROUGH THE FAITH OF CHRIST, THE RIGHTEOUSNESS WHICH IS OF GOD BY FAITH**:

Note—The parallel with Rom 3:21-26 is unmistakable, and the Primary Meaning of the genitive 'OF God, OF Christ' is *stated undeniably* as source or origin. If there is the slightest doubt that this is the *personal* Faith of God and Christ, this puts an end to it:

Col 2:11-12 In whom also ye are circumcised with the circumcision made without hands, in putting off the body of the sins of the flesh by the circumcision of Christ: 12 Buried with him in baptism, wherein also ye are risen with him **through the faith of the operation of God**, who hath raised him from the dead.

Note—Again, the parallel with Rom 3:21-26 is unmistakable, and the Primary Meaning of the genitive Faith OF God is undeniably source or origin...*because the verse SAYS God OPERATES it!*

★ Gal 2:16,20 Knowing that **a man is not justified by the works of the law, but by <u>the faith OF Jesus Christ</u>**, even <u>**we have believed**</u> in Jesus Christ, <u>**that we might be justified**</u> by <u>**the faith OF Christ**</u>, and not by the works of the law: for by the works of the law shall no flesh be justified....20 I am **crucified** with Christ: nevertheless I live; yet not I, but Christ liveth in me: and **the life which I now live in the flesh I live by <u>the faith OF the Son of God</u>**, who loved me, and gave himself for me.

1. The parallel with Rom 3:21-26 and Col 2:11-12 is unmistakable, and the Primary Meaning of the genitive OF Christ is undeniably source or origin, and it is repeatedly affirmed.
2. "Might be justified" is in the Conditional Subjunctive mood in both English and Greek, supporting and restating Paul's argument in Rom 3:21-26 that our faith merely *manifests* the pre-existing condition that God has *already* justified us.
   Also, this is mutually supportive with the Parallel Passage 1 Jn 5:1. Amazingly, right in the context, v20 *clearly SAYS it*.
3. The fact of the Crucifixion proves this is Eternal Salvation, and that it comes through the Faith OF Christ, not the faith of the sinner.

★Gal 3:14,22,26 That the blessing of Abraham might come on the Gentiles **through Jesus Christ; that we might receive the promise of the Spirit through faith**....22 But the scripture hath concluded all under sin, **that the promise by <u>faith OF Jesus Christ</u> might be given to them that believe**....26 For **ye are all the children of God by faith in Christ Jesus**.

1. Notice the continued and repeated parallel thought from comparing the Parallel Passages Rom 3:21-26; Phlp 3:8-9; Col 2:11-12; and Gal 2:16,20. Jew and Gentile both receive the Abrahamic Blessing thru the Faith OF Christ on that Cross, and that is the primary meaning of the genitive case, source or origin.
2. Again, the Conditional Subjunctive mood is used in those passages to make it clear that, "Whosoever believeth that Jesus is the Christ is born of God" (1 Jn 5:1).
3. Vs 26—All these interconnected points make it abundantly clear that "faith IN Jesus Christ", *in this verse*, can mean nothing other than IN Jesus *as source or origin (not our*

faith placed in Him as an objective). Notice the *exact same parallel* in

> 1Tm 1:14 And the **grace** of our Lord was exceeding abundant with **faith** and love **which is <u>in</u> Christ Jesus**.

Note that just as surely as the grace and love *must* be that of Christ Jesus, so *must* the faith be His; and that infallibly confirms the faith of Gal 3:26 to be faith *originating* IN Christ Jesus *as its source or origin*.

And that is keeping it as simple as possible, but not any simpler—just by *carefully* hobbling along with a Brain Crutch. That is why you first make sure you *know* what The Bible *says*—because It *means* what it *says*. Now, pick up any of the new modern revised bibles, and check out how they...*phrase*...these passages. As I warned you before (p. 75), some of them have obscured, and most of them have simply obliterated these passages. They have replaced the Doctrine of Eternal Salvation by Grace through Faith OF God and Christ, with the heresy of Neo-gnosticism—Eternal Salvation through the Free Will, Faith, and Works of the Sinner. Remember I showed you that God *prophesied* it would be this way:

> 1 Tim 4:1 Now the Spirit speaketh expressly, that **in the latter times** some shall **depart from the faith, giving heed to seducing spirits, and doctrines of devils**;

Remember how we started with Rom 3, The Righteousness of God by Faith of Jesus Christ? Well, Rom 4 summarizes this concept from Rom 3, by using the example of the Faith of our father Abraham:

> Rom 4:2-5,13-16 For if Abraham were justified by works, he hath whereof to glory; but not before God. 3 For what saith the scripture? **Abraham believed God, and it was <u>counted</u> unto him <u>for</u> righteousness.** 4 Now to him that worketh is the reward not reckoned of grace, but of debt. 5 But **to him that worketh not, but believeth on him that justifieth the ungodly, <u>his faith is counted for righteousness</u>**....13 For the promise, that he should be the heir of the world, was not to Abraham, or to his seed, through the law, but **through the righteousness of faith**. 14 **For if they which are of the law be heirs, faith is made void, and the promise made of none effect**: 15 Because the law worketh wrath: for where no law is, there is no transgression. 16 **Therefore it is <u>of faith</u>, that it might be <u>by grace</u>; to the end the promise might be sure to all the seed**; not to that only which is of the law, but to that also which is of the faith of **Abraham; who is the father of us all**,

1. Vss 3-4. Human Faith is a *token* of Grace, because without Grace there could be no Human Faith.
2. Vss 12-14. Righteousness comes thru the Covenant Faith of the Godhead, not by the sinner keeping commandments.
3. Vs 16. God's Covenant Faith guarantees eternal salvation to every one of God's Elect (the Seed)—Therefore it is <u>of faith</u>, that it might be <u>by grace</u>; to the end the promise might be sure to all the seed. Here is a Parallel Passage that says the same as vs 16:

   > Eph 2:8-10 **For by <u>grace</u>** [Gk. feminine] **are ye <u>saved</u>** [Gk. noun form is masculine] **through <u>faith</u>** [Gk. feminine]; **and that** [Gk. neuter] **not of yourselves: it is the gift of God**: 9 **Not of works, lest any man should boast.** 10 For we are his workmanship, **created in Christ Jesus unto good works**, which God hath before ordained that we should walk in them.

   a. In Greek, Grace and Faith are feminine nouns, Salvation (noun form) is masculine, but the word 'that' is neuter. Why, you reckon?
   b. Because, in Greek grammar, when a list of nouns is referred to with a pronoun, usually the most frequent gender is used, which would normally be feminine in this case. However, to emphasize all nouns *equally*, the neuter is used to refer to the *whole list*, as here. Thus, all three—Grace, Salvation, and Faith—are <u>each</u> *the gift of God*. "Not <u>of</u> yourselves" proves the point using the genitive; *each* of the three—Grace, Salvation, *and Faith*—ARE "*NOT <u>OF</u> YOURSELVES*."
   c. I have shown you how the Doctrine is in the King James English; I have shown you how the Doctrine is in the *Textus Receptus* Greek; now, check out all these passages in the Roman Catholic Manuscripts and all the new modern revised bibles. Notice how...*different*...these passages are from the same ones in the King James Bible and Its underlying Greek. WHY, you reckon?

Over 30 years ago, a friend that I converted gave me a paper, from a famous southern religious university, that listed over 20 different types of genitive case, and suggested that the *dative* genitive could be used to change most Faith OF God and Faith Of Christ verses to Faith IN God and Christ, making them *our free will*. I have given you sufficient information here for an intelligent 10 year old to make an informed decision about *that* (by the way, if someone whispers in your ear that it was Bob Jones University, you did not get that from me).

Tell you what, let's summarize this entire section with *just one* Parallel Passage, taken with the words and grammar in Primary Meanings, forming pretty much a Proof Text of everything we have discussed. Oh, and one more thing...the underlying Hebrew Masoretic Text both *says* and *means* EXACTLY the same thing as the King James English.

Faith OF God and Christ

Psa 89:1-8,19,24,26-34 I will sing of the mercies of the LORD for ever: with my mouth will **I make known thy <u>faithfulness</u> to all generations.** 2 For I have said, Mercy shall be built up for ever: **thy <u>faithfulness</u> shalt thou establish in the very heavens**. 3 **I have made a <u>covenant</u> with my chosen**, I have sworn unto David my servant, 4 Thy seed will I establish for ever, and build up thy throne to all generations. Selah 5 And the heavens shall **praise** thy wonders, O LORD: **thy <u>faithfulness</u> also in the congregation of the saints.** 6 For who in the heaven can be compared unto the LORD? who among the sons of the mighty can be likened unto the LORD? 7 God is greatly to be feared in the assembly of the saints, and to be had in reverence of all them that are about him. 8 O LORD God of hosts, **who is a strong LORD like unto thee? or to thy <u>faithfulness</u> round about thee?**...

19 Then thou spakest in vision to **thy holy one**, and saidst, I have laid help upon one that is mighty; I have exalted one chosen out of the people....24 But **my <u>faithfulness</u> and my mercy shall be <u>with him</u>**: and in my name shall his horn be exalted....26 **He shall cry unto me, Thou art my father, my God**, and the rock of my salvation. 27 Also **I will make him my firstborn, higher than the kings of the earth.** 28 My mercy will I keep for him for evermore, and **<u>my covenant</u> shall stand fast with him**. 29 **<u>His seed</u> also will I make to endure for ever**, and his throne as the days of heaven. 30 If his children forsake my law, and walk not in my judgments; 31 If they break my statutes, and keep not my commandments; 32 Then will I visit their transgression with the rod, and their iniquity with stripes. 33 **<u>Nevertheless</u> my lovingkindness will I not utterly take from him, nor suffer my <u>faithfulness</u> to fail. 34 <u>My covenant</u> will I not break, nor alter the thing that is gone out of my lips.**

Regeneration *before* Faith

John 3:3-8 Jesus answered and said unto him, Verily, verily, I say unto thee, **Except a man be <u>born again</u>, he <u>cannot see</u> the kingdom of God.** 4 Nicodemus saith unto him, How can a man be born when he is old? can he enter the second time into his mother's womb, and be born?

5 Jesus answered, Verily, verily, I say unto thee, **Except a man <u>be born of water and of the Spirit</u>, he cannot enter into the kingdom of God. 6 That which is born of the flesh is flesh; and that which is born of the Spirit is spirit. 7 Marvel not that I said unto thee, Ye must be <u>born again.</u> 8 <u>The wind bloweth where it listeth</u>, and thou hearest the sound thereof, but canst not tell whence it cometh, and whither it goeth: <u>so is every one that is born of the Spirit</u>.**

Titus 3:5-7 **<u>Not</u> by works of righteousness which we have done**, but according to his mercy he saved us, **by the washing of regeneration, and renewing of the Holy Ghost**; 6 <u>Which he shed on us abundantly through Jesus Christ our Saviour; 7 That being justified by his grace, we should be made heirs according to the hope of eternal life.</u>

1 Jn 5:1a <u>Whosoever</u> **believeth** that Jesus is the Christ **is born** of God...

Now, let's talk about our Faith IN God, and how it is related to Regeneration (being born again). John 3 tells us *That* we must be born again, Titus 3 tells us *How* it is done, and 1 John tells us how to know *When* it has been done—we are *able* to believe. Let's look at each Proof Text a little more closely.

<u>Ye must be born again, John 3</u>. FIRST, look at what Christ says, "Except a man be born again, he *cannot see* the kingdom of God." Neo-gnosticism tells us we must *first* choose God so He can *then* eternally save us. Jesus Christ says we must *first* be eternally saved before we can *even see* what it is all about, let alone believe it. That backward stuff sounds familiar, doesn't it? How about: "Ye shall *surely* die"..."Ye shall *not* surely die." *How did that work out?* NEXT, Jesus says, "Born of the water and of the Spirit." What does that mean? The water birth is being born from your mother's womb—God does not eternally save anybody *until* they have first been conceived. Because of Original Sin, in the Garden, His elect are born sinners, then at some point of time pleasing to Him, God *regenerates* an elect person—they are born of the Spirit. In the Beginning, God made His elect children holy. Then, Satan murdered them putting them into sin, thus they are all born into sin. God eternally saves His elect by

regenerating them, *out* of sin and back *into* holiness. Remember the coats of skin God gave Adam and Eve—blood sacrifice of an Innocent, so what had become the sin of their nakedness might be covered? FINALLY, "The wind bloweth *where it listeth* (where *it* wills)." Hurricane Katrina and Hurricane Patricia blew in *when* they wanted to, didn't they? Then, they blew across the country *wherever* they wanted to, didn't they? And they destroyed and flooded whatever they wanted to, didn't they? *Who controls the Winds?*

> Job 28:23-28 **God** understandeth the way thereof, and he knoweth the place thereof. 24 For he looketh to the ends of the earth, and seeth under the whole heaven; 25 **To make the weight for the winds; and he weigheth the waters by measure. 26 When he made a decree for the rain, and a way for the lightning of the thunder: 27 Then did he see it, and declare it; he prepared it, yea, and searched it out.** 28 And unto man he said, Behold, the fear of the Lord, that is wisdom; and to depart from evil is understanding.
>
> Luke 8:22-25 Now it came to pass on a certain day, that he (Christ) went into a ship with his disciples: and he said unto them, Let us go over unto the other side of the lake. And they launched forth. 23 But as they sailed he fell asleep: and **there came down a storm of wind on the lake; and they were filled with water**, and were in jeopardy.
>
> 24 And they came to him, and awoke him, saying, Master, master, we perish. Then **he arose, and rebuked the wind and the raging of the water: and they ceased, and there was a calm.** 25 <u>And he said unto them, Where is your faith?</u> And they being afraid wondered, saying one to another, **What manner of man is this! for he commandeth even the winds and water, and they obey him.**

When The Bible *says*, "The Wind bloweth where it listeth," what does that *mean*? It *means* that the Holy Spirit, like the wind blowing, breathes regeneration whenever and wherever *HE decides to*, not where the dead alien sinner decides to *let* him blow.

<u>Not by works of righteousness, Titus 3.</u> This parallels the thought of Rom 3 (pp. 78-79), "The righteousness OF God which is by Faith OF Jesus Christ." God, through His mercy, takes His Righteousness, which the Faith OF Christ provided by dying on the Cross according to the Eternal Covenant, and applies it to an elect sinner by the washing of regeneration and renewing of the Holy Ghost, thus giving the elect sinner eternal life. *Not one whit* of the sinner's works of righteousness is involved, and that *specifically excludes* the sinner's faith, which is a work (Rom 9:11; 1 Thss 1:3; 2 Thss 1:11). Yes, I know, lots of people deny these 3 verses define faith as a work. BUT...read what

they *say exactly* in a King James Bible and in the underlying Greek *Textus Receptus* (ignore all those Roman Catholic manuscripts), because that is what they *mean exactly*. Just remember how they play the GRAMMAR GAME: "Ye shall *surely* die"..."Ye shall *not* surely die."

Whosoever believeth, 1 John 5. Notice carefully *When* this verse *says* a person believes—*after* they have been born of God; and "whosoever" *means* no exceptions.

Beyond a doubt *Now*, whenever The Bible *says* Regeneration or Born Again, we know what it *means*. But, *exactly how* is Faith related to Regeneration? There are *only three possibilities*:

1. Faith BEFORE Regeneration—pagan Neo-gnosticism, or Free Will, with our faith as a condition to receiving regeneration.
2. Faith SIMULTANEOUS with Regeneration—John Calvin's favorite fantasy, which he bequeathed to the Presbyterians and their copycats; sometimes called Gospel Means (Calvin brought this out of the Roman Catholic Church, the gospel as a sacrament; which when preached *graciously* enables someone to believe, *if* they decide to); all of which is nothing other than pagan Neo-gnosticism.
3. Faith AFTER Regeneration—*Which we have seen*...is what The King James Bible, and its underlying Hebrew and Greek texts (ignore all those Roman Catholic manuscripts), has been telling us all along.

Let's nail 'Faith AFTER Regeneration' to the bedrock with 5 iron spikes (I *love* doing that—"Prove all things," 1 Thss 5:21). Observe carefully what these 5 Proof Texts *say exactly*, in both *Textus Receptus* Greek and King James English, because that is what they *exactly mean*:

> John 1:12-13 But as many as **received** (aorist tense) him, to them **gave** (aorist tense) he power to become the sons of God, even to them that **believe** (present tense) on his name: 13 **Which were born** (aorist tense passive), **not of blood, nor of the will of the flesh, nor of the will of man, but of God**.
>
> 1. Some helpful definitions—note the *difference*:
>
>   **receive.** be given, presented with, or paid (something).
>   **accept.** consent to receive (a thing offered).
>
>   [Oxford American]
>
>   Note the *difference*: Everyone smacked hard in the face will *receive* it, but very few will *accept* it. See? Receiving Jesus in this verse does *not* mean Accepting Jesus—

these people *received* Jesus when they were born of God...there was no *accepting* to it.

2. The main clause of the sentence is v. 13, *not* v12. It declares as the dominant fact that these people "were born...of God", not of blood (sacrifices), nor will of the flesh (genetic inheritance), nor the will of man (free will, or Neo-gnosticism).

3. Aorist tense in Greek looks at a verb as a finished action, it is equivalent to past tense in English, which is why it was translated that way. *Note very carefully* that these people were born of God (and passive means *God* did it *to* them), thus received the Redemption of Jesus (which is what that logically means, see Rom 3:21-26, p. 78), and were thus given power to become the sons of God (Regeneration), all some time in the past...*all before* they believed (in the present). Faith AFTER Regeneration. From now on, pay close attention to how most preachers *explain* this verse...now that you *know*, ask a few, for the fun of it.

John 5:24 Verily, verily, I say unto you, He that **heareth** my word, and **believeth** on him that sent me, **hath** everlasting life, and shall not come into condemnation; but **is passed** from death unto life.

> Note—Hear, Believe, and Hath are all in the present tense, *all three happening at the same time.* But, Is Passed is in the present perfect tense, meaning that *it happened some time before the present.* Obviously, *before* someone dead in sins can *have* eternal life, they must first *be passed* from death unto life. But, look what that does to *hearing* and *believing*—they are *first* passed from death unto life *before they do that, too.* Faith AFTER Regeneration, you see.

John 17:2-3 As thou hast given him power over all flesh, that **he should** (subjunctive mood) **give eternal life to as many as** thou hast given him. 3 **And this is life eternal, that** (G2443 *ina*) **they might know thee** the only true God, and Jesus Christ, whom thou hast sent.

1. Another example of the Conditional Subjunctive mood: God gave some people to Jesus Christ in the Eternal Covenant, *on condition that* He should give them eternal life, which He did. And Jesus Christ had all the power he needed, over all the flesh there was, so that *not one* of them was lost ('as many as'—every single one).

2. The Gk word *ina*, translated 'that', is a conjunction—a word that connects other words to each other, in this case 'life

eternal' connected with 'knowing' God and Christ. It is used to show the purpose for which something is done:

> **ina**. in order *that* (denoting the *purpose* or the *result*).
> [Strong's Greek Lexicon, *G2443*]

That, you see, is the Primary Meaning of the word *ina*. In addition to giving His People eternal life, according to His Eternal Covenant, God also wants His people to *know* Him and Jesus Christ. Having eternal life makes this possible (which is why atheists are fools and *don't* believe in God, Psa 14:1-3). This verse *states explicitly* that one of the reasons Jesus Christ gives us eternal life is so that *we can know Him and God*. Why? Because, if you don't *know* Them, you cannot *believe* in Them. We are *first* given eternal life by Jesus Christ, so *then* we can *know* and *believe* in Him.

3. There is a GRAMMAR GAME that is played here, to hide the fact Jesus Christ *first* gives us eternal life so that we can *then* believe in Him. *Verse 3 is explained away as if it were a* definition *of eternal life*. Such tricksters say, "This verse *defines* eternal life as 'knowing God and Christ'. IT DOES NO SUCH THING—it explicitly states the *REASON* OR *PURPOSE* for giving eternal life: "That they might know...God and Jesus Christ...". It is true, and I don't deny it, that *part* of eternal life *is* knowing God and Christ, personally and familially; but there is a lot more to eternal life than personal knowledge of God. Notice the GRAMMAR GAME: *It subtly <u>denies</u> the Primary Meaning of* ina (to show reason or purpose) *by <u>claiming</u> that is shows 'definition' instead*...which it does *not*—that is a grammatical error that would flunk you on a Greek 101 pop quiz.

4. You see, what this passage both *says* and *means*, in plain Greek and English, is Faith AFTER Regeneration.

Act 13:48 And when the Gentiles heard this, they were glad, and glorified the word of the Lord: and as many as were ordained (perfect tense passive) **to** (*G1519 eis*) **eternal life believed** (aorist tense active)**.**

> Note—The King James English plainly *says* "as many as were ordained (past perfect tense) to eternal life believed (past tense). The past perfect action takes place *and is finished* before the past action, because it's *even further* in the past. The *Textus Receptus* Greek plainly *says*, "as many as were ordained *into* (which is the Primary Meaning of *eis*) eternal life believed." They *already* had eternal life *when* they believed. Either way, the text plainly *means* Faith AFTER Regeneration.

> 1 John 5:1a **Whosoever believeth** (present tense) that Jesus is the Christ **is born** (perfect tense passive) of God…
>
>> Perfect tense 'is born' (both Gk and Eng) takes place in the past, *before* present tense 'believeth' (both Gk and Eng), and 'whosoever' *means* no exceptions. The verse is a clear Parallel Passage with Act 13:48. Faith AFTER Regeneration.

These 5 passages *alone* are capable of refuting EVERY CONCEIVABLE FALSE RELIGION, even those that haven't been invented yet. You see, ONLY Christianity and Mosaism (Judaism *until* 70 AD) teach Salvation by Grace. All other religions…including Occult Babylonian Talmudism (Judaism *since* 70 AD)…are based upon various systems of Free Will and Works—The sinner FIRST has got to do something or other in order to THEN make it possible for *Some-kinda-higher-power-or-other* to save him (whatever that might mean). Here is how God puts it:

> Rom 9:11,14-16,18 (For **the children** being **not yet born, neither having done any good or evil**, that the purpose of God according to **election might stand, not of works, but of him that calleth**;)…14 What shall we say then? Is there unrighteousness with God? God forbid. 15 For he saith to Moses, **I will** have mercy on whom **I will** have mercy, and **I will** have compassion on whom **I will** have compassion. 16 **So then it is not of him that willeth, nor of him that runneth, but of God that showeth mercy.**… 18 Therefore hath he mercy on whom **he will** have mercy, and whom **he will** he hardeneth.

All conceivable, actual, and historical forms of religion…*without exception*…teach some kinda Free Will and Works for some kinda salvation. ONLY the God of Abraham, *Yehovah Elohim*—I AM, Who is the Divine Nature of The Lord Jesus Christ, eternally saves His Children, enabling Faith AFTER Regeneration. And that is *how* you can know True Religion, beyond any reasonable doubt.

TULIP

T otal Depravity
U nconditional Election
L imited Atonement
I rresistible Grace
P reservation of the Saints

Since the early years of the Protestant Reformation, TULIP has been used as a short form of briefly explaining the Plan of Salvation. **T** explains *Why*, **U** explains *Who*, **L** explains *How*, **I** explains *Cause*, and **P** explains *Effect*. And that explains Eternal Salvation as simply as possible...but not any simpler (Einstein smiles and sticks out his tongue, you've seen the picture). Let's explain and prove each one *sufficiently*, using the 4 Principles and 5 Rules of Bible Study.

TOTAL DEPRAVITY—As a result of Satan murdering Adam and Eve in the Garden of Eden, they and all their children (the *total* number of humanity) are *Depraved* in *all* of their abilities and faculties (*totally*), and thus are *Incapable* spiritually, mentally, emotionally, or physically of approaching unto God savingly.

> **depraved**. morally corrupt; wicked. From Latin *depravare*, from *de-* 'down, thoroughly' + *pravus* 'crooked, perverse.' [Oxford American]
>
> **incapable**. 1 unable to do or achieve (something).
> • not allowing the possibility of (a particular action).
> 2 unable to behave rationally or manage one's affairs; incompetent. [Oxford American]
>
> Psm 14:2-3 The LORD looked down from heaven upon **the children of men**, to see if there were **any** that did understand, and seek God. 3 **They are all gone aside, they are all together become filthy: there is none that doeth good, no, not one**.
>
> Rom 8:7-8 Because **the carnal mind** is enmity against God: for it **is not subject to the law of God, neither indeed can be**. 8 So then **they that are in the flesh cannot please God**.
>
> Eph 2:1b-3 ...**Dead in trespasses and sins**; 2 Wherein in time past ye walked according to the course of this world, according to the prince of the power of the air, the spirit that now worketh in the children of disobedience: 3 **Among whom also we all** had our conversation in times past in the lusts of our flesh, **fulfilling the desires of the flesh and of the mind; and were by nature the children of wrath, even as others**.

Many people believe that Death in The Garden affected only Adam and Eve, but their children are born free of sin, for their own fair shot. Nay, not so:

> Job 25:4 How then can man be justified with God? or **how can he be clean that is born of a woman**?

> Psm 51:5 Behold, I was **shapen** **in iniquity**; and **in sin did my mother conceive me**.
>
> Psm 58:3 **The wicked** are **estranged** **from the womb**: they go astray as soon as they be born, speaking lies.
>
> Rom 5:12-14 Wherefore, **as by one man sin entered into the world, and death by sin; and so death passed upon all men, for that all have sinned**: 13 (For until the law sin was in the world: but sin is not imputed when there is no law. 14 Nevertheless **death reigned from Adam to Moses, even over them that had not sinned after the similitude of Adam's transgression**, who is the figure of him that was to come.

Other folks believe that special people, like Priests and Monks and other Holy Ones can reach out and help save sinners. Sadly, no:

> Psm 49:7-9 **None of them can by any means redeem his brother, nor give to God a ransom for him:** 8 (For the redemption of their soul is precious, and it ceaseth for ever:) 9 That he should still live for ever, and not see corruption.
>
> Note—The *sum total* of *all* the Holy Sacraments *ever* offered, taken together, are worth *less* than a fleck of fly dung, for the saving of even a *single* soul.

This is what Total Depravity finally comes down to:

> Rev 20:12b-14 ...**The dead were judged out of those things which were written in the books, according to their works.** 13 And the sea gave up the dead which were in it; and death and hell delivered up the dead which were in them: and **they were judged every man according to their works. 14 And death and hell were cast into the lake of fire.** This is the second death.
>
> Note—*Every* Dead Man (the *total* number judged) judged according to their Works (and thus the *total* number of their abilities and faculties, that could conceive and perform those Works...whether considered *Good or Bad*) will be cast into Hell Fire. Total Depravity. See?

UNCONDITIONAL ELECTION—God in Eternity, foreseeing the Fall of Adam and Eve, elected them and all of their Children—the Woman's Seed, who would have been born *had there been no Sin* —to be eternally saved from Sin *solely* through the Work of Christ and *not* through any condition, will, or work they might *conceivably* perform. *All* of the Extra People, being Satan's Seed

—born *only* because of the Curse, which greatly multiplied Eve's conception—were left in their Sin.

We've already covered this in Eternal Election (p. 65-70), so we will summarize briefly with these verses,

> Psa 14:2-3 The LORD looked down from heaven upon **the children of men**, to see if there were **any** that did understand, and seek God. 3 **They are all gone aside, they are all together become filthy: there is none that doeth good, no, not one**.
>
> Rom 8:7-8 Because **the carnal mind** is enmity against God: for it **is not subject to the law of God, neither indeed can be**. 8 So then **they that are in the flesh cannot please God.**
>
> Note—These two passages *completely devastate* the Neo-gnostic Roman Catholic fairy tale that God elected those He foresaw from eternity would accept Christ if they only had a chance...THERE WEREN'T ANY, BECAUSE THEY CAN'T!
>
> Eph 1:3-4 Blessed be the God and Father of our Lord Jesus Christ, who hath blessed us with all spiritual blessings in heavenly places in Christ: 4 **According as he hath chosen us in him before the foundation of the world**, that we should be holy and without blame before him in love:
>
> Gen 3:14-16a And **the LORD God said unto the serpent**, Because thou hast done this, thou art cursed above all cattle, and above every beast of the field; upon thy belly shalt thou go, and dust shalt thou eat all the days of thy life: 15 And **I will put enmity between thee and the woman, and between THY SEED and HER SEED; it shall bruise thy head, and thou shalt bruise his heel.**
> 16 Unto the woman he said, **I will greatly multiply** thy sorrow and **thy conception**;

One last thing...How *many* are eternally chosen? As Christians must, we turn to our Jewish Beginnings for the answer:

> Isa 6:11-13 Then said I, Lord, how long? And he answered, Until the cities be wasted without inhabitant, and the houses without man, and the land be utterly desolate, 12 And the LORD have removed men far away, and there be a great forsaking in the midst of the land.
> 13 But yet **in it shall be a TENTH, and it shall return**, and shall be eaten: as a teil tree, and as an oak, whose

substance is in them, when they cast their leaves: **so the holy seed shall be the substance thereof.**

ONE TENTH of the Jews are eternally saved, they are the Woman's Seed, and are written in The Lamb's Book of Life. Nine tenths of the Jews are going to be judged out of the Books according to their works on Judgement Day, they are Satan's Seed. Notice what I have told you before—After the Captivity, the majority of Elect Jews returned to the Land, the majority of non-elect Jews remained in Babylon (v13). In 70 AD, God destroyed the Nation for the sin of killing The Messiah. The Jewish historian Josephus tells us when Jerusalem fell, 1.1 million Jews were killed, and 97 thousand were taken captive. I think most of that tenth of the Jews who survived were Elect...I served a church in Las Vegas for 27 years...*wanna bet?* One thing I do know for sure. Since then, Judaism has ceased to be Mosaism, and ever after has been nothing but Occult Babylonian Talmudism. Gee...*reckon why?*

How many elect Gentiles? Let's keep following those Jewish roots. Read carefully 1 Cor 10:1-4, comparing Jews to Gentiles; there it all is. For the lazy reader, here come the gorilla fingers again, one for each nostril:

> 1 Cor 10:6-7a, **Now these things were our examples** [*tupos, G5179*], to the intent we should not lust after evil things, as they also lusted. 7a Neither be ye idolaters, as were some of them...11 **Now all these things happened unto them for ensamples** [*tupos, G5179*]: and they are written for our admonition, upon whom the ends of the world are come. 12 Wherefore let him that thinketh he standeth take heed lest he fall.
>
> **tupos**. a *die* (as *struck*), that is, (by implication) a *stamp* or *scar*; by analogy a *shape*, that is, a *statue*, (figuratively) *style* or *resemblance*; specifically a *sampler* ("type"), that is, a *model* (for imitation) or *instance* (for warning). [*G5179*, Strong's Greek Lexicon]
>
> **type**. 2 a person or thing symbolizing or exemplifying the ideal or defining characteristics of something
> 5 *Theology* a foreshadowing in the Old Testament of a person or event of the Christian tradition.
> [Oxford American]

Since the Jews are a *type* for Gentiles (Paul writing down the *exact* words God *spoke* to him, and God letting *none* of them fall to the ground), and since *one-tenth* of the Jews are elect, we may logically conclude that *one-tenth* of the Gentiles are elect. So...there is the whole human race, since The Fall: 10% Woman's Seed, 90% Satan's

Seed—her conception *greatly* multiplied. Now...consider the whole stupid history of the human race, from Sin in the Garden until now. Next, consider the history of the nation of Israel, up to 70 AD, then ever after. Finally, consider the history of the *Constitutional Republic* our predominantly King-James-Bible-believing Founding Fathers gave us, 'til we lost it in 1865 from the Sin of Slavery (the North selling, the South buying—*both* guilty), then compare the *Politically-correct Crapola 'Democracy'* the Babylonian Banking Families (who financed the Lincoln administration and *every* administration since) have given us. Looked at *this* way, all the stupidity *finally* makes sense. TWO SEEDS...*One* first, with a gift from God; then after Sin corrupts, followed by the *Other*, suborning and perverting the gift—10% inevitably failing through Sin, 90% inevitably prevailing through Sin. See?

LIMITED ATONEMENT—Christ died *only* for those written in The Lamb's Book of Life—The Woman's Seed...but, for *none* of those judged out of the Books according to their works—Satan's Seed.

> John 6:37-39 **ALL that the Father giveth me** shall come to me; and him that cometh to me I will in no wise cast out. 38 For I came down from heaven, not to do mine own will, but the will of him that sent me. 39 **And this is the Father's will which hath sent me, that of ALL which he hath given me I should lose nothing, but should raise IT up again at the last day**.

> Matt 1:20-21 But while he thought on these things, behold, the angel of the Lord appeared unto him in a dream, saying, Joseph, thou son of David, fear not to take unto thee Mary thy wife: for that which is conceived in her is of the Holy Ghost. 21And **she shall bring forth a son, and thou shalt call his name JESUS: for he shall save HIS PEOPLE from their sins.**

> Eph 1:4, 7 According as **he hath chosen US in him before the foundation of the world**, that we should be holy and without blame before him in love...7 **In whom WE have redemption through his blood, the forgiveness of sins, according to the riches of his grace**;

> Rom 8:28-33 And we know that all things work together for good to them that love God, to them who are **the called according to his purpose.** 29 For whom he did foreknow, he also did predestinate to be conformed to the image of his Son, that he might be the firstborn among many brethren. 30 Moreover whom he did predestinate, them he also called: and whom he called, them he also justified: and whom he justified, them he also glorified.

31 What shall we then say to these things? If God be for us, who can be against us? 32 **He that spared not his own Son, but <u>delivered him up for us all</u>** ['us all' *WHOM*? Read on...], **how shall he not <u>with him</u> also freely give us all things?** 33 Who shall lay any thing to the charge of **GOD'S ELECT**? It is God that justifieth.

Rev 20:11- And I saw a great white throne, and him that sat on it, from whose face the earth and the heaven fled away; and there was found no place for them. 12 And I saw the dead, small and great, stand before God; and the books were opened: and **another book was opened, which is <u>the book of life</u>**: and the dead were judged out of those things which were written in the books, <u>according to their works</u>....15 **And whosoever was <u>not</u> found written in <u>the book of life</u> was cast into the lake of fire.**

Primary Meanings, Proof Texts, Parallel Verses...*Praise God from Whom all Blessings flow!* THAT is How to Study The Bible.

IRRESISTIBLE GRACE—God's Amazing Grace (**G**od's **R**iches **A**t **C**hrist's **E**xpense) are poured out from the Death of Christ on the Cross, upon God's Elect *but dead* Children, by the Holy Spirit; *irresistably* giving them *both* Eternal Life and *all* spiritual Abilities, so they might *know* their Heavenly Father and their Redeemer.

Ezk 16:4-9 [God speaking to Jerusalem, v3] And as for **thy nativity, in the day thou wast born** thy navel was not cut, neither wast thou washed in water to supple thee; thou wast not salted at all, nor swaddled at all. 5 None eye pitied thee, to do any of these unto thee, to have compassion upon thee; but **thou wast cast out in the open field, to the lothing of thy person, in the day that thou wast born.**
      6 <u>And when I passed by thee, and saw thee polluted in thine own blood, I said unto thee when thou wast in thy blood, Live; yea,</u> **I said unto thee when thou wast in thy blood, <u>LIVE</u>.** 7 I have caused thee to multiply as the bud of the field, and thou hast increased and waxen great, and thou art come to excellent ornaments: thy breasts are fashioned, and thine hair is grown, whereas thou wast naked and bare.
      8 <u>Now when I passed by thee, and looked upon thee, behold, thy time was the time of love</u>; and **I spread my skirt over thee, and covered thy nakedness: yea, I sware unto thee, and entered into a covenant with thee, saith the Lord GOD, and thou becamest mine.** 9 **THEN** washed I thee with water; yea, I thoroughly

washed away thy blood from thee, and I anointed thee with oil.

Tit 3:3-7 For we ourselves also were sometimes foolish, disobedient, deceived, serving divers lusts and pleasures, living in malice and envy, hateful, and hating one another. 4 <u>But after that</u> the kindness and love of God our Saviour toward man appeared, 5 **Not by works of righteousness which we have done, <u>but according to his mercy he saved us, by the washing of regeneration, and renewing of the Holy Ghost;</u>** 6 Which he shed on us abundantly through Jesus Christ our Saviour; 7 That <u>being</u> justified by his grace, we should be <u>made</u> heirs according to the hope of eternal life.

John 17:1-3 These words spake Jesus, and lifted up his eyes to heaven, and said, Father, the hour is come; glorify thy Son, that thy Son also may glorify thee: 2 **As thou hast given him <u>power over all flesh</u>, that he should <small>GIVE</small> eternal life <u>to as many as thou hast given him</u>.** 3 And this is life eternal, <small>THAT</small> **they might <small>KNOW</small> thee the only true God, and Jesus Christ, whom thou hast sent.**

Col 2:13-14 **And you, being dead in your sins** and the uncircumcision of your flesh, **hath he quickened together with him**, <u>having forgiven you all trespasses; 14 Blotting out the handwriting of ordinances that was against us, which was contrary to us,</u> and **took it out of the way, nailing it to his cross;**

Primary Meanings, Proof Texts, Parallel Verses...The Word of God in The Words of God. My goodness!... How *irresistible* is it, when God Himself does it?

Dan 4:35 And all the inhabitants of the earth are reputed as nothing: and **he doeth according to his will** in the army of heaven, and among the inhabitants of the earth: **and <u>none</u> can stay his hand, or say unto him, What doest thou?**

PRESERVATION OF THE SAINTS—best defined by The Word of God in The Words of God:

Psa 37:28 For **the LORD** loveth judgment, and **forsaketh not his saints; they <u>are PRESERVED for ever</u>:** but <u>the seed of the wicked</u> shall be cut off. [Note—Two Seeds!]

Jude 1: Jude, the servant of Jesus Christ, and brother of James, **to them that are sanctified by God the Father, and <small>PRESERVED</small> in Jesus Christ,** and called:

> **saint**. a person acknowledged as holy or virtuous and typically regarded as being in heaven after death. [Oxford American]

These two Proof Texts correct another boo-boo by John Calvin, who believed in the *Perseverance* of the saints...but, there is *not one verse* in a King James Bible about saints *persevering* forever. John Calvin was *heretically* enamored by the Roman Catholic doctrine of Sacrament of the Preached Word—believing it to *instrumentally* bestow saving grace, so believers could *persevere*. Quite to the contrary, check this out:

> Psa 89:26-34 **He shall cry unto me, Thou art my father, my God**, and the rock of my salvation. 27 Also **I will make him <u>my firstborn</u>, higher than the kings of the earth.** 28 My mercy will I keep for him for evermore, and **<u> my covenant</u> shall stand fast with him**. 29 **<u>His seed</u> also will I make to endure for ever**, and his throne as the days of heaven. 30 **<u>If his children forsake my law, and walk not in my judgments; 31 If they break my statutes, and keep not my commandments; 32 Then will I visit their transgression with the rod, and their iniquity with stripes.</u>** 33 **<u>Nevertheless</u> my lovingkindness will I not utterly take from him, nor suffer my <u>faithfulness</u> to fail. 34 <u>My covenant</u> will I not break, nor alter the thing that is gone out of my lips.**

I have taught you How to Study The Bible, so you tell me: Does this *MEAN* Preservation *or* Perseverance? Also, remember the two Proof Texts I showed you above...*which SAY it*. In the mouth of two witnesses shall every word be established (cp. 2 Cor 13:1b; Deut 19:15; and Matt 18:16). John Calvin's Presbyterian System is *partially* right, which unfortunately means that *doctrinally* it is all wrong. Remember, Jesus was baptized by a Baptist preacher, so He was *not* a Methepisco-*terianatholi*-campbellitormon (see above, pp. 73-74).

TULIP, the Plan of Salvation. God *chose* Abraham, the progenitor of the Jews, who were God's *chosen* people; Christ was the *Chosen One*, the Jewish Messiah; He built His Church upon *chosen* Jewish apostles. *Who do you think True Christians will be?* God's Saving Grace was planted in an Abrahamic bulb, which produced a Jewish stalk, and flowered into a TULIP...See? Let's just trace that out in the next Core Doctrine of Christianity.

Tent of Abraham, Tabernacle of Moses, Church of Christ

This is the doctrine (systematic teaching) of the *Public* Worship of *Yehovah Elohim*, the True God Whom we identified in the first Core Doctrine (see pp. 62-65). Now we are going to identify the True Worship of That True God; which *necessarily implies* that ALL OTHER 'worships' of ALL OTHER 'gods' are FALLACIOUS—the coming *inclusive* One World Religion of the United Nations *decidedly to the contrary*.

In the world before The Flood, God had no *formalized public worship*. He had a True Worship, but it was not public for everyone— it was private, held in the family tents of a line of Patriarchs, those whose bloodline would eventually produce The Seed of The Woman. That line was: Adam ⇒ Seth ⇒ Enos ⇒ Cainan ⇒ Mahalaleel ⇒ Jared ⇒ Enoch ⇒ Methuselah ⇒ Lamech ⇒ Noah (The Flood) ⇒ Shem ⇒ Arphaxad ⇒ Salah ⇒ Eber ⇒ Peleg ⇒ Reu ⇒ Serug ⇒ Nahor ⇒ Terah ⇒ Abram (Abraham)—10 patriarchs *before* The Flood, including Noah; and 10 patriarchs *after* The Flood, down to Abraham.

The Patriarchs had a very simple form of worship composed of a designated sacrifice, made at a designated place, and at a designated time (all designated by the patriarch), accompanied by the Patriarch briefly reminding his family what God had promised to the family line.

> Gen 4:2-5 And she again bare his brother Abel. And Abel was a keeper of sheep, but Cain was a tiller of the ground. 3 And **in process of time it came to pass**, that **Cain brought** of the fruit of the ground an offering unto the LORD. 4 And **Abel, he also brought** of **the firstlings of his flock and of the fat thereof.** And the LORD had respect unto Abel and to his offering: 5 But unto Cain and to his offering he had not respect. And Cain was very wroth, and his countenance fell.

Designated Sacrifice—"Firstlings of the flock and the fat thereof"; Designated Place—Cain and Abel "brought"; Designated Time—"in process of time it came to pass." And why, do you reckon, an animal blood sacrifice?

> Gen 3:21 Unto Adam also and to his wife **did the LORD God make coats of skins, and clothed them.**

It was because Adam, the first Patriarch, told his family what God did to forgive them, and how God explained it to them, in the Beginning. And please notice this an all-important Truth: *God* found them both naked, *God* made the coats of skin (and thus killed the animal), and

God put the coats upon both Adam and Eve—a simpler picture of TULIP cannot be drawn...even a toddling child can understand.

In the family worship, the Patriarch showed his children *What God Did*, using the firstlings of the flock; then he told them *What God Said*, passing down the Promises. This is generally called Patriarchal Worship. It prevailed before and after The Flood, until God formalized His Public Worship for the first time, through Moses.

There was other information, no doubt conveyed and preached by the Patriarchs, based upon the stars and constellations...*and the meaning of their names*.

> Gen 1:14 And God said, **Let there be lights in the firmament of the heaven** to divide the day from the night; **and let them be for signs, and for seasons**, and for days, and years:
>
> Note—A **sign** is a portent or omen, particularly of things to come. A **season** may be a time of the year, such as spring or fall; or "properly an appointment, that is, a fixed time or season" (see Strong's H4150).
>
> Psa 147:4 He **telleth the number** of the stars; **he calleth them all by their names**.
>
> Note—**Telleth** means to count, as a bank teller. All stars with **names** were *originally named by God* (tho' devils and men may *change* those names!)—and never forget, Bible names *mean* something.
>
> Job 38:31-32 Canst thou bind the sweet influences of Pleiades, or loose the bands of Orion? 32 **Canst thou bring forth Mazzaroth in his season?** or canst thou guide Arcturus with his sons?
>
> Note—**Bring forth** is Qal construction in Hebrew, and indicates *causation*: "cause to bring forth." **Mazzaroth** is Strong's H4216; both Strong and Briggs, Driver, and Brown tell us that it means, "the 12 signs of the Zodiac and their 36 associated constellations." **Season** indicates an appropriate time or time period; in this case the annual procession of the rising sun, appearing to move sequentially through the 12 major signs of the zodiac.

These passages are talking about *Astronomy*, particularly Bible Astronomy. Please give serious attention to these passages; note what they *say*, and especially what they *don't* say—they *never* say or imply "astrology".

Astrology is a form of divination and fortune telling, and as such is condemned as a sin (Deut 18:9-14 and others)...remember, I said men and devils *changed* some of the star and constellation names—*and* they changed the whole purpose of the *Mazzaroth*, also. Under Nimrod in ancient Sumer (Gen 10-11, during the days of the patriarch Peleg, 2247-2008 BC), this form of early astrological divination was incorporated into the first state religion. Over the centuries, following the scattering from the Tower of Babel, this demonized drivel became the Babylonian Mystery Religion. It was the prime ingredient—called the *Prisca Theologica*, the Ancient Religion—of much subsequent ancient religions, the scattered peoples taking it with them all over the world. Note very carefully—The early Sumerians, and the Fallen Angels they worshipped as gods (known to them as *Anunnaki*), adopted and bastardized the Astronomy of the Patriarchs into Astrology...Abraham and his descendants DID NOT adopt and Hebraize the Astrology of the Sumerians. Astrology, and the worship of the *Anunnaki* as gods, constituted the first post-Flood Revised Satanic Version (RSV) of God's True Religion.

The *Mazzaroth*—the Signs of the Zodiac—were created by God in the Beginning; and the 12 major constellations, with their 36 minor constellations, including a number of stars within them, were all *named* by God. These *names*, as well as the *forms* of the constellations, were *Signs*—prophetic portents—of the Coming of The Seed of The Woman (fulfilled 2 BC-33 AD). It is from these *names* that we learn the most doctrine, not necessarily from the pictures of them. In the first sign, Virgo (The Virgin), we see a Woman holding Seed in her hands (The Seed of The Woman). The following signs then proceed in a determined sequence, foretelling what we now perceive to be events in the Life of Christ. The final sign is the Lion, triumphant over the Serpent beneath His feet. Jesus was The Lion of the Tribe of Judah, ascended to Rule in Heaven (Rev 5). The lion was the symbol of the Tribe of Judah, from which Christ descended (Gen 49:8-12).

Obviously, the Patriarchs did not have the *details* of prophecy, which those who have read the Life of Christ in the New Testament now possess. But, they knew The Seed of The Woman would come; they knew He would battle the Serpent, be wounded in the heel, but crush the Serpent's head; they knew He would be a great Deliverer; they knew He would finally become King. How did they know? Adam, the First Patriarch, experienced the Fall in the Garden, and heard God pronounce the Promise and the Curse with His Divine Mouth. Adam was *shown by God* how a sacrificed animal could provide a symbolic covering, and Adam thereafter *showed his family*, as the designated time, place, and manner of offering confirm. *And God named the stars, and told the names to Adam.* And Adam passed these things down the line of patriarchs to Abraham, with whom God made a Covenant—and began His *formal public worship* in the Tent of Abraham.

Years ago I preached a sermon series on this topic entitled Bible Astronomy. I recommend two excellent sources: **The Gospel in the Stars** by Joseph A. Seiss, and **The Witness of the Stars** by E. W. Bullinger. Both are excellent in dealing with the *Names* of the stars and constellations. Beware of Bullinger, though...he's a Dispensationalist (we will deal with *that* in the last Core Doctrine).

In 1921 BC, 427 years after The Flood and 2,083 years after Creation, God made a COVENANT WITH ABRAHAM (for the most accurate Biblical Chronology I know, see Dr. Floyd Nolan Jones' **The Chronology of the Old Testament**).

First, and of supreme importance, God *had already* brought Abraham out of Ur of the Chaldees. This delivered him from the *damnable* Occult Babylonian Mystery Religion...which the majority of Jews would fall back into during the Captivity...and which is known today as Occult Babylonian Talmudism. Abrahamism, Mosaism, and Christianity are all "come out of" religions—"come out of" all the pagan crapola around you, as God called Abraham to come out of Ur of the Chaldees, and worship the True God with the True Religion. Why do you reckon the Pope in Rome and the United Nations *both* want an INCLUSIVE religion? Think about it.

With the Abrahamic Covenant, God modified Patriarchal Worship, into what I am calling the Tent of Abraham. God narrowed the Promised Bloodline to Abraham's descendants *only* (specifically through Isaac then Jacob); God required the males of the family to be circumcised; God allowed *circumcised* Friends of the Family to participate in worship; God praised Abraham for commanding his household to keep the Way of The Lord. Later, Jacob added the offering of a tenth of first fruits to God. Almost all of these modifications God would later command Moses to codify in The Law. Thus, the Tent of Abraham was *Yehovah Elohim*'s True Worship for the last 430 years of the Patriarchal age, until Moses and the Exodus from Egypt. Here are the highlights:

> Gen 15:1,4-10,17-18 After these things the word of **the LORD came unto Abram in a vision**, saying, Fear not, Abram: I am thy shield, and thy exceeding great reward.... 4 And, behold, the word of the LORD came unto him, saying...**he that shall come forth out of thine own bowels shall be thine heir.** 5 And he brought him forth abroad, and said, Look now toward heaven, and tell the stars, if thou be able to number them: and he said unto him, So shall thy seed be. 6 And he believed in the LORD; and he

counted it to him for righteousness.

7 And he said unto him, **I am the LORD that <u>brought thee out</u> of Ur of the Chaldees**, to give thee this land to inherit it. 8 And he said, Lord GOD, whereby shall I know that I shall inherit it? 9 And he said unto him, Take me **an heifer of three years old, and a she goat of three years old, and a ram of three years old, and a turtledove, and a young pigeon.** [Note—5 types of sacrificial animals, that Moses later codified] 10 And he took unto him all these, and divided them in the midst, and laid each piece one against another: but the birds divided he not.....

17 <u>And it came to pass, that, when the sun went down, and it was dark, behold a smoking furnace, and a burning lamp that passed between those pieces.</u> 18 **In the same day the LORD made a <u>covenant with Abram</u>, saying, Unto thy seed have I given this land, from the river of Egypt unto the great river, the river Euphrates:**

Gen 17:7,10,13-14 And **I will establish my covenant between me and thee and thy seed** after thee in their generations for an everlasting covenant, to be a God unto thee, and to thy seed after thee....10 This is my covenant, which ye shall keep, between me and you and thy seed after thee; **Every man child among you shall be circumcised** [later codified by Moses]....13 He that is born in thy house, and he that is bought with thy money, must needs be circumcised: **and my covenant shall be in your flesh for an everlasting covenant.**

14 And the uncircumcised man child whose flesh of his foreskin is not circumcised, that soul shall be cut off from his people; he hath broken my covenant.

Gen 18:17,19 And the LORD said, Shall I hide from Abraham that thing which I do...19 **For I know him, that he will command his children and his household after him, and they shall keep the way of the LORD, to do justice and judgment** [later codified by Moses]; <u>that the LORD may bring upon Abraham that which he hath spoken of him.</u>

Gen 28:10-13,20-22 And Jacob went out from Beersheba, and went toward Haran. 11 And he lighted upon a certain place, and tarried there all night, because the sun was set; and he took of the stones of that place, and put them for his pillows, and lay down in that place to sleep. 1 2And he dreamed, and behold a ladder set up on the earth, and the top of it reached to heaven: and behold the angels of God ascending and descending on it. 13 And, behold, the

LORD stood above it, and said, I am the LORD God of Abraham thy father, and the God of Isaac: the land whereon thou liest, to thee will I give it, and to thy seed...

20 **And Jacob vowed a vow, saying**, If God will be with me, and will keep me in this way that I go, and will give me bread to eat, and raiment to put on, 21 So that I come again to my father's house in peace; then shall the LORD be my God: 22 And this stone, which I have set for a pillar, shall be God's house: **and of all that thou shalt give me I will surely give the tenth unto thee** [later codified by Moses].

Thus was Patriarchal worship REFORMED INTO the Tent of Abraham. There are three interesting things to note about this Tent of Abraham. First, God begins to allow non-family to participate in the formal worship, *provided they are circumcised*. This was later codified by Moses as part of Tabernacle worship. And, it was a type of Baptism, which would still later be required for membership and formal worship in the Church. Second, Tent of Abraham became the *structural* outline for the Tabernacle of Moses, when God expanded it into a very complex form of Public Worship under Moses. Third, when God finally came to earth in the person of The Lord Jesus Christ and REFORMED the Tabernacle of Moses into the Church of Christ, the Tent of Abraham would be the *conceptual* outline for the Church (more about this in a minute). THUS WE SEE HOW THE TRUE GOD FORMALLY DEVELOPED HIS TRUE WORSHIP FIRST INTO TENT OF ABRAHAM, THEN INTO TABERNACLE OF MOSES, AND FINALLY INTO CHURCH OF CHRIST. In the first two cases, God personally told chosen men what to do; and in the last case, He came and *did it Himself*.

When God brought the Jews out of Egypt in 1491 BC, He commanded Moses to REFORM His formal worship *for the first time* into openly Public Worship, in a specified place—The Tabernacle (later under David and Solomon in a Temple patterned after The Tabernacle), and in a greatly expanded and detailed manner. This REFORMATION of His True Worship, God maintained for 1561 years, until the Destruction of Israel in 70 AD. Since virtually everybody the world over *knows* the Tabernacle of Moses was God's True Worship among the Jews (whether they *believe* it or not), there is not much point in proving the obvious.

John 1:17 For THE LAW was given by Moses...

Gal 3:19, Wherefore then serveth THE LAW? **It was added** because of transgressions, **till <u>the seed</u> should come to whom the promise was made**; and it was ordained by angels in the hand of a mediator....24 Wherefore THE LAW was our schoolmaster to bring us unto **Christ**, that we might be justified by faith.

Finally, The Seed of The Woman did come (review pp. 47-50)—The Lord Jesus Christ...His human nature born of a virgin, *conjoined* with the Second Person of the Trinity, The Word (I AM Himself, review pp. 62-65). One of the many things Jesus Christ did was to RE-FORM God's True Worship into it's third and final form (three, the number of the Trinity)—just as His Divine Nature had *already* done TWICE BEFORE:

> Matt 16:15-18 He saith unto them, But whom say ye that I am? 16 And Simon Peter answered and said, **Thou art the Christ, the Son of the living God.** 17 And Jesus answered and said unto him, **Blessed art thou, Simon Barjona: for flesh and blood hath not revealed it unto thee, but my Father which is in heaven.** 18 And I say also unto thee, That thou art Peter, and **upon this rock I will build my church; and the gates of hell shall not prevail against it.**

> Heb 9:1-2a,8-12,15 Then verily THE FIRST COVENANT had also ordinances of divine service, and a worldly sanctuary. 2 For there was a **tabernacle** made…
> 8 The Holy Ghost this **signifying**, that **the way into the holiest of all was not yet made manifest, while as the first tabernacle was yet standing: 9 Which was a figure for the time then present**, in which were offered both gifts and sacrifices, that could not make him that did the service perfect, as pertaining to the conscience; 10 Which stood only in meats and drinks, and divers washings, and carnal ordinances, imposed on them **until the time of REFORMATION.**
> 11 **But Christ being come** an high priest of good things to come, by **a greater and more perfect tabernacle**, not made with hands, that is to say, not of this building; 12 Neither by the blood of goats and calves, but **by his own blood he entered in once into the holy place, having obtained eternal redemption for us.**…
> 15 And for this cause **he is the mediator of THE NEW TESTAMENT**, that by means of death, for the redemption of the transgressions that were under the first testament, they which are called might receive the promise of eternal inheritance.

And it is amazing to observe how God *extended* the essence of the Tent of Abraham, *structurally* all through the Tabernacle of Moses, and *conceptually* into the Church of Christ—showing how *all three* are sequential *forms* of the *one* True Worship of God. This is explained in Romans 4; here are the essential excerpts:

> Rom 4:1-5,9-12,16-17,23-25 What shall we say then that Abraham our father, as pertaining to the flesh, hath found? 2 For if Abraham were justified by works, he hath whereof to glory; but not before God. 3 For what saith the scripture? **Abraham believed God, and it was counted unto him for righteousness.** 4 Now to him that worketh is the reward not reckoned of grace, but of debt. 5 But **to him that worketh not, but believeth on him that justifieth the ungodly, his faith is counted for righteousness**....
>
> 9 Cometh this blessedness then upon the **circumcision only, or upon the uncircumcision also**? for we say that faith was reckoned to Abraham for righteousness. 10 **How was it then reckoned? when he was in circumcision, or in uncircumcision? Not in circumcision, but in uncircumcision. 11 And he received the sign of circumcision,** A SEAL OF THE RIGHTEOUSNESS OF THE FAITH WHICH HE HAD YET BEING UNCIRCUMCISED: **that he might be** THE FATHER OF ALL THEM THAT BELIEVE, **though they be not circumcised;** THAT RIGHTEOUSNESS MIGHT BE IMPUTED UNTO THEM ALSO: 12 And the father of circumcision to them who are not of the circumcision only, but who also walk in the steps of that faith of our father Abraham, which he had being yet uncircumcised....
>
> 16 **Therefore it is of faith, that it might be by grace; to the end the promise might be sure to all the seed; not to that only which is of** THE LAW, **but to that also which is of** THE FAITH OF ABRAHAM; **who is the father of us all,** 17 (As it is written, I have made thee A FATHER OF MANY NATIONS,) before him whom he believed, even God, who quickeneth the dead, and calleth those things which be not as though they were....
>
> 23 **Now it was not written for his sake alone, that it was imputed to him; 24 But for us also, to whom it shall be imputed, if we believe on him that raised up Jesus our Lord from the dead; 25 Who was delivered for our offences, and was raised again for our justification.**

1st, Note the words *counted, reckoned,* and *imputed*. These are three English synonyms translating the same Greek word—*G3049 logizomai* = to *take an inventory*, that is, *estimate* (literally or figuratively). This is an accounting term, dealing with the Sin debt and its payment, and illustrates the Doctrine of Imputation: The Seed of The Woman *pays* that debt, with His Life on that awful Cross;

and then God through the Holy Spirit *applies* that payment (counts, reckons, imputes) to all of the Elect—*so they can then Believe in Him and Rejoice*...dancing and singing, as it were, in a field of TULIPS. Faith AFTER Regeneration, you see.

2nd, Father Abraham was thus a figure, or *type*, of ALL Believers, *both* Jew *and* Gentile. JUST AS he was *first* given eternal life by God, *then* manifested it by the sign of Faith and Circumcision; JUST SO all Jewish Elect do likewise, and all Gentile Elect as well, but with the sign of Faith and Baptism.

3rd, observe how the Conditional Subjunctive (review pp. 76-81 , 85-88) is used to state this. Note that some Condition was done by God (The Blessedness was given) in order that an effect MIGHT follow (Abraham's Faith and Circumcision). Follow that word "might" all the way through Rom 4...there is the Conditional Subjunctive, in plain sight. You do so need that Brain Crutch—which is why the government schools took it away 50 years ago, and why I am trying to give it back...*IF...you are able*...to accept it.

4th, Notice how the elements of the Tent of Abraham were REFORMED by God, *first* into the Tabernacle of Moses for His Elect Jewish Children, *then* into the Church of Christ for His Elect Gentile Children, "To the end the Promise might be sure to ALL THE SEED," so that Abraham might be "The Father of circumcision to them who are *not* of the circumcision *only*, but who *also* walk in the steps of *That Faith of our father Abraham, which he had being yet uncircumcised*."

God's True Worship in all ages, from Adam to Christ—Tent of Abraham, Tabernacle of Moses, Church of Christ. And remember, Christ was baptized by a man He four times called "John the *Baptist*". Therefore, CHRIST WAS A BAPTIST; and the Church He founded was of *logical necessity* BAPTIST...*any other* conclusion is *grammatically erroneous* and *logically asinine* (review pp. 73-75, 96 ¶4). The Last Supper proves The Church was *fully functional* in 33 AD. The Methepiscoterianatholicampbellitormon Church did *not* make its *first* enduring appearance until 325 AD...292 YEARS LATER...proclaimed into existence by the *heathen* Emperor Constantine, possessing all of the elements of the Mystery Religion of Babylon (*Prisca Theologica*), and *declared* to be the Roman Catholic Church. Even that name is a stupid heathen contradiction. First, it *supposed* to be the Church *of Christ*, not of Rome. Second, if it is *catholic* (meaning "universal"), how can it be only Roman? Third, if it is *Roman*, how can it be catholic? Stupid...heathen...contradiction.

You think I am making all of this up? *Really? After all of those Bible verses* THAT SAY IT? Then maybe *you* should *verify* this asserted origin of the Roman Catholic Church *yourself,* by reading **The Two Babylons, or The Papal Worship proved to be the Worship of Nimrod and his Wife**, by Alexander Hislop. Two things about this book. 1) It is a scholarly treatise, *not* an easy read. 2) *Every single point is Proven.* To verify the origin and history of the Baptist Church as the Church of Christ, I recommend **The Trail of Blood**, by J. M. Carroll. It is a small book, in outline form, with an excellent historical chart. Just right for an overview, with all the essentials you need to know. For those readers who like to nail things down with an iron spike (as I do), study **A Concise History of Baptists**, by G. H. Orchard. A full length book laid out like Trail of Blood, by the sequence of centuries...the two fit each other like interlaced fingers. There is a *reason* why Jesus said, "John the BAPTIST". It's the *same* reason His Church has been called ANABAPTIST ("again-baptist", because they were "come-outers" of *everything* else) and BAPTIST, down through all the centuries since it was *reformed* out of the Tabernacle of Moses. *Because...*THAT'S WHAT IT IS.

Amillennialism vs. *all* other -isms

NOTE CAREFULLY THE CHRONOLOGICAL SEQUENCE
OF THE FOLLOWING EVENTS:

THE ASCENSION OF CHRIST, 33AD
Act 1:6-11 When they therefore were come together, they asked of him, saying, <u>Lord, wilt thou at this time restore again the kingdom to Israel?</u> 7 And he said unto them, **It is not for you to know the times or the seasons, which the Father hath put in his own power.** 8 <u>But ye shall receive power, after that the Holy Ghost is come upon you: and ye shall be witnesses unto me both in Jerusalem, and in all Judaea, and in Samaria, and unto the uttermost part of the earth.</u>

    9 And when he had spoken these things, **while they beheld, he was taken up; and a cloud received him out of their sight.** 10 And while they looked stedfastly toward heaven **as he went up**, <u>behold, two men stood by them in white apparel; 11 Which also said, Ye men of Galilee, why stand ye gazing up into heaven?</u> this same **Jesus, which is taken up from you into heaven**, <u>shall so come in like manner as ye have seen him go into heaven</u>.

CHRIST IN TRANSIT 33 AD, *BETWEEN* EARTH AND HEAVEN
Rev 4 then Rev 5:1-4 And **I saw in the right hand of him**

that sat on the throne a book written within and on the backside, sealed with seven seals. 2 And I saw a strong angel proclaiming with a loud voice, Who is worthy to open the book, and to loose the seals thereof? 3 And **no man in heaven, nor in earth, neither under the earth** [the *only* place left in the universe is *in transit* COJ], was able to open the book, neither to look thereon. 4 **And I wept much, because no man was found worthy to open and to read the book, neither to look thereon.**

CHRIS ENTERS HEAVEN, *AFTER* HIS TRANSIT, AND IS CROWNED WITH HONOR AND GLORY, 33 AD

Rev 5:5-7,11-13 **And one of the elders saith unto me, Weep not: behold, the Lion of the tribe of Juda, the Root of David, hath prevailed to open the book, and to loose the seven seals thereof.** 6 And I beheld, and, lo, in the midst of the throne and of the four beasts, and in the midst of the elders, **stood a Lamb as it had been slain**, having seven horns and seven eyes, which are the seven Spirits of God sent forth into all the earth. 7 **And he came and took the book out of the right hand of him that sat upon the throne.**...

11 And I beheld, and I heard the voice of many angels round about the throne and the beasts and the elders: and the number of them was ten thousand times ten thousand, and thousands of thousands; 12 Saying with a loud voice, **Worthy is the Lamb that was slain to receive power, and riches, and wisdom, and strength, and HONOUR, AND GLORY, and blessing.** 13 And every creature which is in heaven, and on the earth, and under the earth, and such as are in the sea, and all that are in them, heard I saying, **Blessing, and HONOUR, AND GLORY, and power, be unto him that sitteth upon the throne, and unto the Lamb for ever and ever.**

CHRIST *AFTER* THE ASCENSION, ~62-64 AD

Heb 2:7-9 **Thou madest him a little lower than the angels; thou CROWNEDST him with GLORY AND HONOUR, and didst set him over the works of thy hands: 8 Thou hast put all things in subjection under his feet.** For in that he put all in subjection under him, he left nothing that is not put under him. But now we see not yet all things put under him. 9 But **we see Jesus, who was made a little lower than the angels for the suffering of death, CROWNED with GLORY AND HONOUR; that he by the grace of God should taste death for every man.**

CHRIST'S STATUS, FROM 33 AD UNTIL HIS SECOND COMING
Rev 1:10,12-13,17-18,3:21-22 I was in the Spirit on the Lord's day, and heard behind me a great voice, as of a trumpet,...12 And I turned to see the voice that spake with me. And being turned, I saw seven golden candlesticks; 13 And in the midst of the seven candlesticks one like unto the Son of man, clothed with a garment down to the foot, and girt about the paps with a golden girdle....17 And when I saw him, I fell at his feet as dead. And he laid his right hand upon me, saying unto me, Fear not; I am the first and the last: 18 **I am he that liveth, and <u>was dead</u>; and, behold, I am alive for evermore, Amen**; and have the keys of hell and of death....3:21-22 **To him that overcometh will I grant <u>to sit with me IN MY THRONE</u>, even as <u>I also overcame, and am set down with my Father in his throne.</u>** 22 He that hath an ear, let him hear what the Spirit saith unto the churches.

The Word of God in The Words of God—The Lord Jesus Christ ascended into Heaven in 33 AD, was Crowned with Glory and Honor, then sat down in His Throne, with His Father in His Throne, and has been reigning IN HIS *MILLENNIAL* KINGDOM ever since. His 1,000 year reign has been going on now (2015) for 1,982 years. See?

This is why it's called *A-millennialism—Christ's 1,000 year reign takes place from the* HEAVENLY *Jerusalem, NOT from the* EARTHLY *Jerusalem—*AND TIME FLOWS...*DIFFERENTLY*...IN HEAVEN.

2 Pet 3:8 But, beloved, <u>be not ignorant of this one thing</u>, that **one day is with the Lord as a thousand years, and a thousand years as one day**.

Now, we all know that is a metaphor. But, there are two things it teaches that cannot be denied. One, Time in Heaven *runs <u>both</u> ways*: faster *or* slower than on Earth, as God decides. Two, the difference factor, either way, can be up to 165,000 to 1—*because Scripture says so*. Therefore, 1000 = 1982 (so far)...1,000 years in Heaven *but* 1,982 years on Earth. See *now*?

Conclusion: The Correct Bible Doctrine is Amillennialism (Christ's 1000 year reign takes place from the Heavenly Jerusalem, *not* the Earthly Jerusalem); *any and all other -isms,* including Dispensationalism, that teach Christ's 1000 year reign takes place on Earth, in earth time, *are heresy*. Sample:

"The Old Testament prophet saw in one horizon, so to speak, the suffering and the glory of Messiah...The New Testament shows that His suffering and glory *are separated by the present Church Age* [my emphasis, COJ], and

> points forward to the Lord's return as the time when the Davidic Covenant of blessing through power will be fulfilled... [New Scofield Reference Bible, "The Four Gospels"]

Oh, pooh. You have a clear choice: The King James Bible, which declares that Christ ascended into Heaven, was Crowned with glory and honor, and is set down in His Throne with His Father in His Throne —*with Christ Himself saying it*...OR...The Scofield Reference Bible, and all forms of Dispensationalism, *denying it*. Choose wisely...*but first*...consider what happens when Christ Returns:

> 1 Cor 15:24-26 Then cometh **the end**, when he shall have delivered **up** the kingdom **to God**, even the Father; when he shall have put down all rule and all authority and power. 25 For **he must reign**, till he hath put all enemies under his feet. 26 The last enemy that shall be destroyed is **death**.

Please notice carefully what the passage *says*, so that you can know what it *means* (because it *means* what it *says*). It *says* 5 things:

> **1st**, When Christ returns, it will be the *End*, not the beginning, of His Reign...and also the End of everything else.
>
> **2nd**, Christ will return and *deliver up* His Kingdom, not start it *down* here on earth.
>
> **3rd**, Christ will return and deliver up His Kingdom *to God The Father*, not set it up on earth for anyone else.
>
> **4th**, Christ is not returning to reign...*He is reigning already*.
>
> **5th**, When Christ returns there will be *The* Resurrection... *JUST one*...*NOT two* with 1000 years between (Act 24:15 ... There shall be **A** resurrection of the dead, **BOTH** of the just and unjust.).

I repeat, you have a clear choice: The King James Bible and Amillennialism...OR...The Scofield Reference Bible and all forms of Dispensationalism—*which denies all 5 points*. Choose wisely.

But, it gets better.

Jesus Christ was always saying stuff. Too much stuff. He never could just let well enough alone, for some folks. For instance, He said two things *too much* about this 'dispensational' stuff and the End of the World...too much for Dispensationalists, that is. Let's see how that works.

Christ and His Disciples were talking one day about the Temple. This conversation has been called The Olivet Discourse (found in

Matt 24:1-44; Mark 13:1-37; Luke 21:5-36). Christ commented, "There shall not be left here one stone upon another, that shall not be thrown down. (Matt 24:2; also cp. Mark 13:2 and Luke 21:6)" That stirred the pot, because Jews of that time (we know from their writings) believed the Temple would stand until the End of Time. So, the Disciples asked Him three simple questions: "Tell us, when shall these things be? and what shall be the sign of thy coming, and of the end of the world? (Matt 24:3)" His answer, *to those three questions*, was the Olivet Discourse.

The answer to the first question, the destruction of the Temple, took place about 40 years later, in 70 AD. We *now* know, there have been 1878 years, from then until the answers to the last two questions *began*...with the Jewish Return to the Land in 1948. Remember those last two questions: What shall be the sign of Your Coming, and of the End of the World? It was while answering those last two questions, that Jesus said two things *too much* for the Dispensationalists:

> Luke 21:23-24 But woe unto them that are with child, and to them that give suck, in those days! for there shall be great distress **in the land,** and wrath **upon this people.** 24 And they shall fall by the edge of the sword, and shall be led away captive into all nations: [happened in 70 AD] and **Jerusalem shall be trodden down of the Gentiles, until the times of the Gentiles be fulfilled.** [happened in 1948]

> Luke 21:31-33 So likewise ye, when ye see these things come to pass, know ye that the kingdom of God is nigh at hand. 32 **Verily I say unto you, This generation** [one *Last* Generation, beginning in 1948...] **shall not pass away, till all be fulfilled.** [...with *everything fulfilled* during that Last Generation...] 33 **Heaven and earth shall pass away:** [...and then the End of the World...*during* that Last Generation] **but my words shall not pass away.**

- First thing *too much*—The Times of the Gentiles *ended* in 1948, the only Bible time remaining is The Last Times (which *includes* Christ's Second Coming *and* the End of the World).

- Second thing *too much*—The Last Times will last *exactly one Last Generation* after 1948 (and *include* Christ's Second Coming *and* the End of the World).

What's the point? *There ain't no time* for no more time...and there *especially* ain't no time for no 1000 years *more* time, in which to have an *earthly* millennial dispensation. Two things *too much*. Too bad, so sad. "Now the Spirit speaketh expressly, that in the latter times some shall depart from the faith, giving heed to seducing spirits, and doctrines of devils (1 Tim 4:1)"...and to Scofield Reference Bibles.

Well, how *much* time, then? Since 1948? *How much time*, in that Last Generation?

There are three generations mentioned in The Bible, that might apply to what Christ called "this generation", during which "heaven and earth shall pass away," which we must identify with a Bible generation; because of Principle #2 of Bible Study, Proof Texts and Reference Texts; and because of Rule #2 of Bible Study that says, Compare all Cross-references or Parallel Passages on a given topic.

> Psa 90:10a The days of our years are **threescore years and ten**; and if by reason of strength they be **fourscore years**...

> Isa 65:20 There shall be no more thence an infant of days, nor an old man that hath not filled his days: for the child shall die **an hundred years old**; but the sinner being **an hundred years old** shall be accursed.

Three generations, identified with life spans, from The Bible. Which one best fits the time left, since 1948, when the Jews Returned to the Land? Remember, the Return to the Land was historically *motivated* by the Slaughter of 6 million Jews in the prison camps of Nazi Germany, which we know *began* in 1940. So, the Return *logically began* in 1940, and was *fait accompli* by 1948. I choose to count, therefore, from 1940, because *I cannot believe* that the Slaughter of 6 Million Jews *means nothing* in the scheme of things. 70 years, the normal lifespan, doesn't fit: 1940 + 70 = 2010—it's 2015 as I write, and heaven and earth are still *here* (last time I looked). That leaves 1940 + 80 = 2020, and 1940 + 100 = 2040. Both *might* fit, which one fits *best*?

Remember carefully that what Christ said *exactly* was, "Verily I say unto you, **THIS GENERATION** SHALL NOT PASS AWAY, TILL **ALL** BE FULFILLED. Heaven and earth shall pass away... (Luke 21:32-33)" This is important, because what Christ MEANT *exactly*, was *exactly* what He SAID.

There are several...*THINGS*... that **ALL** must be fulfilled. Among them are: The Calling Up of the Two Witnesses (Rev 11:1-13), The Great Tribulation (Rev 7:9-14), The Last Destruction of Jerusalem (Zech 12:9-14; 13:7-9), The Catching Up of All Elect who are Alive and Remain (1 Thss 4:13-18), and the serpentine coils of The Battle of Armageddon which will destroy all the nations of the world (too many references to list here, but start with Zec 12:9 together with Rev 16:12-16). Of the two generational endings left (2020 and 2040), which one *best* can accommodate *All* these remaining things that *must be fulfilled*?

I will admit that God can cram jam an amazing amount of stuff into 5 years, if He wants to. He made the entire universe in 6 *days*. And look what He crammed into 3 *and a half years* in 66-70 AD. But pertinent verses *say* that He is gathering the nations using the Devil (cp. Zech 12:9; Rev 20:7-9; Rev 16:12-16)...and *deluded* devils and *fumbling* human governments move almighty slow. So, to me, all these necessary things (and others we just haven't mentioned) make 2020...*less likely*.

Which leaves 2040 (and about 25 years remaining) at the outside. Even the fallacious Scofield Bible shows these remaining events *could* easily fit into 7 years (whether they *actually* will or not), in which case we have *over three times* more time remaining than needed. Personally, I do not think it will take three times longer than needed. I could be wrong, that's just my opinion. But remember, those deluded devils and fumbling human governments *are being butt-kicked along by God*...Who *can* get things done, when He is a-mind to.

Just look at the Middle East, where everybody knows the Battle of Armageddon *will* take place. Israel and the Jews are in the middle of it; with Iran swearing to blow Israel off the face of the earth; with Obama and NATO trying their best to make a treaty with Iran to *guarantee* them a bomb in 10 years to do it with; with Russia bombing the crap outta the Islamic Fundamentalists (which America, Saudi Arabia, United Arab Emirates, and Qatar *have recruited and supplied* to do their dirty work—getting a gas pipeline built from Qatar...*through Syria*...to Europe, to cut Russia out of that market); and lastly note, that ALL THE MAJOR PLAYERS HAVE NUCLEAR WEAPONS! Do people really think that the Battle of Armageddon is going to take another 25 years to get started? *Really?* What are they *smoking*, with their heads stuck up there, in their butts?

Just for fun, let's take the 7 years even the Scofield Reference Bible admits is all that is really needed for the windup, and add it to 2015 (which is when I'm writing this), then we get 2022—which puts us *into* the last 100 year generation. The Battle of Armageddon is *the SLOWEST moving piece of Stuff that's got to happen* (and NATO has already shot down a Russian fighter bomber, and killed the parachuting pilot *with American-supplied weapons*). God is the One mostly moving the Other Stuff. He only used 6 days to *start* the universe. He claims He is going to end it IN ONE DAY. What if God sorta *sprinkles* everything else in, a bit at a time, while Armageddon *slops* together... then...BOOM?

Will that fit? Will that fit *best*? Jesus said only the Father knoweth the day and the hour *these things* will be, but that *they all* will fit into that Last Generation (Matt 24:34-36).

One thing I believe we can *logically* agree upon—Dispensationalism, in *any* form, *won't* fit...AT ALL. And at this point in time, Time has become the whole point.

Summary

This brings to a close our discussion concerning the 7 Core Doctrines. A lot more could be said about each of these, I have only outlined them, as any Bible student can see. But, this isn't a book about Bible Doctrine...it's a book about How to Study The Bible. I summarized the 7 Core Doctrines to illustrate the application of the 4 Principles and 5 Rules of Bible Study.

My secondary purpose was to help focus any Bible student on *where* to start serious Bible Study, and *what* to build upon. I do not believe there is any better such foundation than these 7 Core Doctrines.

In Conclusion,

> EITHER you can believe The Word of God in The Words of God, studied out Definitionally, Grammatically, and Logically— and confirm It with archaeologically validated historical material (less than 10% of the human race has *ever* done this).
>
> OR you can ignore The Bible, and believe any fairy tale you choose (over 90% of the human race has *always* done just that).

IT REALLY IS JUST THAT SIMPLE.

Isa 40:8 The grass withereth, the flower fadeth: but THE WORD OF OUR GOD shall stand for ever.

*****

Chapter 4—Bible Study & Reading (Tools and Tips)

First Things First
Good Tools for Bible Study
Bible Reading Tips

First Things First

Study and Reading are two different things. Trying to do both simultaneously is like trying to cook an egg sunny side up and scrambled at the same time. Bible Study is for analyzing words and grammar, and developing your understanding of Doctrine. We have already covered those subjects. Bible Reading, which this section will cover below, is more like going for the history and the story line, or devotional reading in books like Proverbs and Psalms. I'll give you some helpful tips on Reading The Bible, that others taught me.

It helps to set a regular time and place for prayer and Bible study or Bible reading. Choose a place where you can keep all your books, paper, and pencils, so you won't loose valuable time or break your concentration having to stop and fetch something. Try to read at the same time each day, and allow at least 15-30 minutes, so you can get something worthwhile done. Start and finish with prayer, and don't permit interruptions. If the phone rings, you're not home. If it's important, they will call back—30 minutes won't stop the world. If you have a regular reading time and place set aside, it will help set your mood and 'kick-start' your brain. Nothing else will accomplish as much. Trust me on this one.

Good Tools for Bible Study

For *really serious* Bible students, it is necessary to inform you about **Hazardous Materials**, by Gail Riplinger (*1,203 pages*), a graduate level text book by a tenured professor of literature. It is subtitled *Greek and Hebrew Study Dangers*. There has always been, since the Garden of Eden, a serious effort by Satan to pervert, revise, change, distort, and deny The Words of God in The Word of God. Some of the *best* Bible study tools of the last 100 years have been *subtly shifted away* from a King James Version approach, even misdirecting the unwary from the underlying Masoretic Hebrew and *Textus Receptus* Greek. Some of the *best* tools were even written by perverts, like heretics and homosexuals and pedophiles. "Good Lord!", you say, "Why do you still use stuff like that?" Because...sad to say...*those tools are some of the best*. We are living in the Last Times (see Amillennialism, pp. 106-113). Things have gotten *so* bad, that some of the best Bible Study tools are only the best of *The Bad*. It will get worse. It will get *much* worse. *READ RIPLINGER'S BOOK.*

Remember the Garden. Remember the Fruit. *Remember the Voice that suggested* it. We have come to the point that some of the best we have got to eat are rotten bananas. Peel the whole fruit first. Then break off the useful parts from the rotten spots. Even then, when you bite in and find...*wiggly things*...don't swallow. *You done been told.*

A BRAIN CRUTCH (see pp. 10-11)

A GOOD STUDY BIBLE

This is of prime importance. I recommend you pay good money for this. A good quality Bible will outlast a cheap one by years. The best one I know is a **Thompson Chain-reference Bible**. It is not cheap—leather covers and good quality Bible paper will cost $80-90, or more, but it will last for years. The notes are *excellent*, and almost entirely non-denominational, which is a very rare thing, trust me. Maps, book outlines, and all, they are very helpful. Many prefer just Bible text, and there is nothing wrong with that...but as I said, buy quality. You'll never regret it.

Another thing—get an inexpensive Bible case; naugahyde is good, so is nylon. Keep your Bible in that case *at all times* it is not in use. It will protect your expensive study Bible from spills, drops, heat, weather, tiny kids, pets, and similar 'evils', and literally add years to the life of your Bible. I used to wear Bibles out every 3-5 years 'til I learned this trick. I have been using my present Bible for over 25 years—it do make a difference!

The future has come! You might want to go digital. If you have an Apple iPhone, iPod Touch, or an iPad, take a llloooooonnng look at the Mantis Bible Study app. It's a mind blower. I use it. You can add-on an astonishing number of fine books (and tons of fluff, too, if you like that stuff). But ask around. There are several other outstanding apps.

A GOOD ENGLISH DICTIONARY

If you don't know what words *mean*, how can you possibly understand what words *say*? Also, remember that the King James Version was translated in 1611. *Some* words have changed meaning, and *all* words have added meanings since then—BUT THE WORDS OF GOD IN THE WORD OF GOD HAVE NOT. You need a dictionary that will make it easy to find the meanings used in 1611. Obviously, the translators did not intend meanings that did not even exist at the time! Your dictionary should arrange the definitions chronologically—*most dictionaries do not do this!* The best dictionary is one of the shorter editions of the **Oxford English Dictionary.** It will run you around $50 to $150, but the definitions are in chronological order with dates, giving you virtually a King James dictionary. This is the dictionary other than which, there is none whicher.

Since I wrote the last paragraph years ago, Oxford Press has seen fit to screw this dictionary up. They arbitrarily inserted time periods instead of dates, and even spraddled the 1611 with a longer period that makes it impossible to *precisely* date KJV words now. It is useless for that. *I do not believe this was unintentional.* See if you can find an older edition on Alibris or AddALL, two fine book finders. If you can't find it, then any of the following is better and cheaper than the new Oxford screw-up.

To get as close as possible to the KJV meanings, a reprint of the **Noah Webster 1828 Dictionary** is hard to beat. Don't pay an ungodly sum for the facsimile edition. Hunt around for an edition less than $20. If you read from an iPad, iPod or iPhone, it adds on to the Mantis Bible Study app; and probably to some of the other apps. For about $17 from Amazon, most people will probably prefer the **Webster's New World College Dictionary** (I have both). The definitions are in chronological order, but are not dated. Pay careful attention to the etymology and the first couple of definitions, and you're right on, in most cases. What about the few other cases, you ask? About $50-150 more for that old Shorter Oxford, that's what!

A GOOD BIBLE DICTIONARY & ENCYCLOPEDIA

The trouble with Bible dictionaries is, so many of them are being published by liberals. A golden oldie that has recently been brought out in an updated edition is **Davis' Dictionary of The Bible.** Another is **Smith's Bible Dictionary.** You can get a good one with the Mantis Bible Study app. They are fairly inexpensive (about $15) and keyed to the King James Version. If you want to go in style, try **Zondervan's Pictorial Bible Dictionary.** It is pricey, but it has pushbutton windows, a stereo, and a 'coon tail' on the radio antenna! There are a number of words in the Bible that have peculiar meanings (like *wimple, an omer is the tenth part of an ephah,* and *Mahershalalhashbaz*). A Bible dictionary will zip right through them. Also, subjects will be summarized and peoples' biographies given in brief. Very handy thing, a Bible dictionary.

If you're going to get that Mantis app, also get the **International Standard Bible Encyclopedia** (ISBE) add-on. Superb. I strongly urge a free standing hard copy of ISBE for *every* serious Bible student. I have the 1939 edition...minimal liberalism. Be cautious with any newer editions. Dictionaries explain *Words*, encyclopedias explain *Subjects*.

A GOOD *EXHAUSTIVE* CONCORDANCE

An *exhaustive* concordance lists every word in the Bible, in alphabetical order, and gives every verse that word appears in. It is *abso-*

lutely invaluable for Bible study. There are two things in particular it will enable you to do: 1) If you can remember even one word in a verse, you can find that verse; 2) You can look up every occurrence of a word, and do thorough subject study, if you need to. Just be sure to get an *exhaustive,* not an abridged, concordance. The very best is a **Strong's Exhaustive Concordance**, with the Greek and Hebrew dictionaries. They are now very reasonably priced. You will find it quite helpful, I assure you. If you are hopelessly strapped for bucks, then get an unabridged **Cruden's Concordance.** It is almost as good (for English), but then "almost" only counts in horseshoes. Of course the Strong's concordances come with the Mantis app mentioned before.

THE SUPER-WOMBAT GOODY

It is called the **Treasury of Scriptural Knowledge**, edited by R.A. Torrey. Get the old classic that's been around forever. *Be careful* of the fancy new editions—they cost a lot more, and they are polluted with the premillennialism and dispensationalism heresies we have just studied.

The Treasury is a collection of well over *500 thousand* parallel passages and verse references, collected over centuries, many of them by the King James Translators, and some dating as far back as the Helvetic Confessions. It is laid out in the form of a commentary, with a summary for each chapter of The Bible. The verses are broken down into subsections, each instead of text having an average of over 38 parallel passages and/or reference verses listed. True, upon reading them, you'll wonder why they put some of them in there; about 2/3 of them will make you more than satisfied you bought the book; *but some of them...*Thank you, Lord!...will be bits of gold *so precious* they will bring tears to your eyes, how they open The Scripture! You see, The Bible is Its own best interpreter—which is why God Himself put those 4 Principles and 5 Rules in There in the first place (see Summary, p. 60). *The Treasury*, like a caring teacher, takes a toddling Child of God by its little hand, and leads it to the most delightful places. One edition comes with that wonderful Mantis app I've been mentioning.

I recommend *every single Christian who reads their Bible everyday* get a *Treasury of Scriptural Knowledge*. For most, it will be the only commentary you will ever need. I have been preaching now for over 50 years. When I started out, ignorant as a chicken, I bought three full length multivolume commentaries, then over a few years, added a couple of bookshelves more of single volume commentaries. After about 5 or 6 years, when I needed a commentary, you know what I wound up using? For about 95% of my serious commentary reading, then 'til now, *The Treasury of Scriptural Knowledge* (along with an Interlinear Bible and Analytical Concordance, which I'll tell you about next). *Nothing* explains The Bible better than The Bible.

HIGHLY TECHNICAL GOODIES

Serious Bible students (and preachers and ministerial students) need to have good Lexicons (dictionaries) of Hebrew and Greek. Think of Strong's lexicons as high school, and the ones I'm going to recommend as college. I recommend versions that utilize the Strong Concordance numbers, to help identify words. Two of the very best, in my opinion, are: J.H. Thayer's **Greek-English Lexicon of the NT**; and Gesenius' **Hebrew and Chaldea Lexicon of the OT**—*both* numerically coded to Strong's Exhaustive Concordance. Two others often used are Liddell and Scott's **Greek-English Lexicon** and **The Brown-Driver-Briggs Hebrew and English Lexicon**. BDB's notes and comments are liberal to the point of suckola; but surprisingly, the definitions themselves are quite good.

Interlinear Bibles and Analytical Concordances, in my opinion, are priceless tools for any *advanced* Bible student; and are *essential* tools for preachers and ministerial students. They enable an English Reader to parse and analyze, with precision, the Hebrew and Greek texts underlying the King James Version. True, some variants also exist that allow one to so analyze *other* Hebrew and *other* Greek texts underlying *newer revised* bibles...but I won't waste your time with interlinear texts or analytical concordances for things of no more inherent worth than a Mickey Mouse comic book (for reasons proven *precisely and thoroughly* in Chapter 1).

INTERLINEAR BIBLES have one line of English, then the next line in either Greek or Hebrew, with corresponding words and phrases matching, so alternating from the beginning to the end. They enable an English Reader to precisely correlate the English text with the corresponding Greek or Hebrew text so translated. The *absolutely most useful* interlinears are the ones that identify the Greek and Hebrew words with their corresponding Strong Concordance numbers.

ANALYTICAL CONCORDANCES list every English word translation, in order, together with the corresponding Greek or Hebrew word (or phrase) so translated, with *a brief grammatical parsing*. This allows an *exact* cross-lingual comparison of Bible words, in English and Greek and Hebrew; and enables precise definition of words with dictionaries and lexicons. Like Interlinear texts, the *most useful* concordances identify the word matches with the corresponding Strong's Concordance numbers.

WHAT TO DO—Lay your King James Bible on the table, along with your proper Interlinear and Analytical Concordance. Then, with your fingers pointing like a little child, you walk through the passage you are studying word by word by word, pausing to make essential notes from time to time. This allows the English Reader to acquire as accurate an understanding of the logical, definitional, and grammatical structure of the underlying text as an *ordinary* reader of the language being studied. It may take 20 minutes using tools, instead of 2 minutes just reading, but...they will get it done...*just as accurately.*

BUT...What if you face CONTENTION from, say, a Doctor (gasp!) who *reads* that language? Not to worry...logically, definitionally, and grammatically you have everything he has got. "But," you sob, "He is a *Doctor!* He understands literary nuances, linguistic clarifications, etymological implications, grammatical intimations, and lots of other stuff I can't even *speelll*!" No sweat. Back up your Strong's lexicon definitions with Thayer and Gesenius (he uses the same, or something not significantly different); get your *Treasury of Scriptural Knowledge* out, and double-check your *very best* Parallel Passages and Proof Texts; *then use your Interlinear text and Analytical Concordance to parse them precisely.* Power in controversy is found in WHAT THE BIBLE *SAYS* AND *MEANS* IN PROOF TEXTS, not in doctoral doo-waddle using graduate level linguistic spoof and piffle. DO IT THIS WAY, and you can jam a gorilla finger up *any* contrary Doctor's nose.

Interregnum:
How to de-Babel Bible Word Definitions

The Biblical Flood occurred in 2348 BC (Biblical Chronology). Satan's One World Socialist Imperium was totally destroyed, and he had to start over from scratch (over 4000 years later, he's finally closing in on it again—watch what happens to fiat paper money, worldwide). If you wish the very best Creationist explanation of How God Did It, get a copy of **In the Beginning**, by Dr. Walt Brown, Ph.D. (Mechanical Engineering, from MIT). Dr. Brown started out to write a paper debunking Creationism, wound up being converted, and has become one of its strongest defenders in our day.

At the Time of The Flood, the earth's crust fractured and collapsed inward, as much as 8-10 *miles* within the Pacific Ring of Fire. This caused the crust to rupture and burst open (popping like a zit), primarily up and down the Atlantic Ocean floor, from North to South (but also ripping open around the world). This caused over 3-1/2% of Earth's mass, including almost all of the massive amount of water contained in the "all the fountains of the great deep" beneath the crustal surface (Gen 7:11), to be ejected from that Atlantic rift and into outer space. Part formed *some* of the cloud of comets that still circle the Solar System, some flew into outer space, but *most* splattered the Moon, and later Mars, like a *devastating* super shotgun blast, before passing on to fall into orbit as the Asteroid Belt (estimated to total only about 3% or so of the Earth's mass—it is *not* a shattered planet). But, a huge portion of the watery mass would not have achieved escape velocity from the Earth's gravity, but would have been quick frozen into ice and snow, then fallen back to the Earth (splattering the *backside* of the Moon on the way back down), causing precipitation of the vast cloud cover which then surrounded the planet (keeping it uniformly warm, so jungles and forests could grow at the North and South poles, which we have found buried and fossilized there). That collapsing cloud cover was "the windows of heaven" which were opened (Gen 7:11). All together, that's where the flood waters came from, and why the *surface* of the Earth is *now* over 70% water.

That is also where *the only ice age this planet ever had* came from; and then lasted about 450-500 years, before it finally melted off around 1900 BC, or so (Job 38:29-30). As this incredible mass of ice melted and ran off the land into the sea, it caused a shift of mass on the already fractured crust, resulting in *yet another* crustal break up. The very few large continents from before the Flood, at some point because of mass-imbalance, shattered and rushed apart, to a new point of approximate mass-balance, forming the configuration of continents we have today (ever notice how you could fit 'em all back together, like a child's jig-saw puzzle? Now you know why). It was *not* Continental Drift (which nobody can yet explain *How*) over millions of years...it was a Hydroplate Event, that happened *mostly* in a day or so. Walt Brown explains *How* in satisfying detail, using scientific mechanisms which have been *confirmed*.

Why are we talking about *this*? Because of Peleg (2247-2008 BC).

> Gen 10:25 And unto Eber were born two sons: the name of one was **Peleg**; **for in his days was the earth divided**; and his brother's name was **Joktan**.

> earth (H776 *'erets*) = From an unused root probably meaning to *be firm*; the *earth* (at large, or partitively a *land*).

> Peleg (H6389) = *Earthquake*. BDB, *Division*.

> Joktan (H3355) = "He will be made little."

Remember Bible Study Principle #1—Primary Meanings. Since the verse is talking about the land surface of the earth (as opposed to the planet itself), we take the Primary Meaning of earth (H776 *'erets*): "partitively a *land*", i.e., the *continents* into which the *land* is divided ("partitive"). If we consider the *meanings* of the words this verse is *saying*, we discover that, In the days of Eber's two sons, the continents (earth) were divided and made little. See? Bible names *mean* something, especially taken in their Primary Meanings. As I said, Walt Brown explains this *very* well. This catastrophic event happened near the end of Peleg's life, probably **around 2050 BC**, give or take.

"But...what's the *point*?" you ask, flapping your arms in frustration. Because *Something Else* happened in Peleg's Days—**The Tower of Babel** (Bible chronology is approximate here, not specific... good inference, from dates that *are* given, **about 2250 to 2200 BC**, or so). That's when Bible Word Definitions got Babel-ed...and we're trying to de-Babel 'em, remember? Here is the Bible account:

> Gen 11:1-9 **And the whole earth was of one language, and of one speech.** [about 100-150 years after The Flood, there would probably be less than 250 thousand people] 2 And it came to pass, as they journeyed from the east, that they found a plain in **the land of Shinar** [Look up Shinar in Wikipedia, then google "map of ancient Shinar"]; and they dwelt there. 3 And they said one to another, Go to, let us make brick, and burn them thoroughly. And they had brick for stone, and slime had they for mortar. 4 And they said, Go to, **let us build us a city and <u>a tower</u>**, whose top may reach unto heaven; and let us make us a name, lest we be scattered abroad upon the face of the whole earth.
>
> 5 And the LORD came down to see the city and **the tower**, which the children of men builded. 6 And the LORD said, <u>Behold, the people is one, and they have all one language; and this they begin to do: and now nothing will be restrained from them, which they have imagined to do. 7 Go to, let us go down, and there confound their language, that they may not understand one another's speech.</u>
>
> 8 **So the LORD scattered them abroad from thence upon the face of <u>all</u> the earth:** and they left off to build the city. 9 Therefore is **the name of it called BABEL; because the LORD did there confound the language of <u>all</u> the earth: and from thence did the LORD scatter them abroad upon the face of <u>all</u> the earth.**

In the days of Peleg (2247-2008 BC), God did *Two Very Important Things*: 1) God *confounded* the One Language into many languages, then He scattered the *entire* human race quickly (about 200 years, at most) across the face of the mostly contiguous land mass; then 2) God *divided* the large continent(s) into 7 much smaller continents, and scattered them apart, as they appear now.

> Act 17: 22a,24a,26b-27 Then Paul stood in the midst of Mars' hill, and said, Ye men of Athens…24 **God that made the world and all things therein, seeing that he is Lord of heaven and earth,**…26…<u>hath made of one blood all nations of men for to dwell on all the face of the earth</u>, and **hath determined the <u>times</u> before appointed, and the <u>bounds</u> of their habitation**; 27 <u>That they should seek the Lord</u>, if haply they might feel after him, <u>and find him</u>, though he be not far from every one of us:

As I said, God doing things in this way *destroyed* Satan's One World Socialist Imperium, and has utterly confounded his attempts to start a new one, for over 4360 years. This was done so *all* of God's Children would have the *opportunity* to seek God and find Him (whether they used it or not). Of course, when the Last Child is conceived, it will be Game Over and Hell to Pay. Some time in the next few years, as this Last Generation dwindles away…

Now, let's de-Babel those Bible Word Definitions. Oh…grab your Brain Crutch (it's on pp. 10-11).

All language, as Aristotle taught us, speaks of just 10 Categories of thinking. 10 Predicables, as he taught it. Everything *Real* must be in one of these 10 categories, either as the subject or the predicate of a declarative sentence. All the parts of speech (such as the 8 Parts of Speech in grammar), in all languages, correspond to one of these 10 categories. They are Substance, Quantity, Quality, Relation, Action, Passion, Place, Time, Posture, Possessing.

Substance is the first Category, and is of supreme importance. All *Real* things are a form of Substance, whether a Holy Angel (spiritual substance) or a lost human sinner (physical substance) or some natural force, like gravity (metaphysical, or non-physical, substance—*careful*…look that word up). Substance is generally expressed by Nouns and Pronouns. They are also the most important part of speech. Everything else, no exceptions, are either something done *by* or done *to* a Noun or Pronoun. Since Pronouns mostly refer to Nouns, *that's* where the action is—Nouns.

The second most important part of speech is Verbs, which express Actions or States of Being. Everything, no exceptions, that Nouns and Pronouns do or can do (or is done to or might be done to them) is a Verb. All Action or Passion (in the sense of passive) is the province of Verbs—and there is nothing else.

Therefore, Nouns and Verbs can *say* all there is to say, about all there *is* to say about. It can be said bluntly and plainly, with just Nouns and Verbs; or it can be said beautifully and precisely, using additionally, all those other parts of speech. But all the Modifiers do is...*modify*...what the Nouns and Verbs *say*. But, either way, there is nothing more to be *said*.

And knowing that is THE KEY TO DE-BABELING.

What I'm going to show you works with any two or more languages; but, as an English Reader, I'm going to stick with English, Hebrew, and Greek...because this is a book about How to Study The Bible. To de-Babel, you have to get back to the Core Meaning, that was clouded and diffused at the Tower of Babel, when the One Language was...*diversified*...to achieve the Confoundation of Goat Boy.

HOW TO DE-BABEL IN 3 STEPS

First, any Word Study that *must* lead to Proof, and *might* lead to Contention, *must* concentrate upon the Nouns and Verbs, and produce de-Babeled definitions that will hold *in all three languages* (imagine a worst case—you're expounding an *English* verse, in which the New Testament *Greek* is quoting Old Testament *Hebrew*—and you are facing...Contention). How do you do that? You *must* first find the Common Core Definition of all *key* trilingual Nouns and Verbs (you *must* de-Babel those key words). Remember all that stuff I was teaching you, before we got sidetracked to Babel? Interlinear Texts, Advanced Analytical Lexicons, and such? *This is where you use them to greatest effect.*

Here is a trick my Mentor, Elder C.E. Smith, Th.D., taught me (please read my acknowledgements to him, to appreciate his qualifications). Venn Diagrams (see Wikipedia) are illustrations, using two or more circles, of the overlap of sets, or categories, of things being discussed. We are going to consider 3 categories: the *commonly shared definition* of *one* key word (Noun or Verb), in English and Greek and Hebrew (eventually we'll want do this with *all* the key words of the verse). Consider three overlapping circles, now concentrate on *that one area where all three overlap*—THAT IS THE COMMON CORE *DE-BABLED* DEFINITION of *that* Bible Word...and *use* that Advanced Analytical Lexicon (for parsing), like a sot drunk uses a jug of moonshine. If you are studying two languages (English and Greek, or English and Hebrew, or Greek and Hebrew) even better, because simpler—it's in that overlap. YOU CONCENTRATE ON THAT COMMON CORE DEFINITION IN THE OVERLAP, and ignore all other possible meanings in either language—*it's just that simple*.

Second, determine the COMMON CORE *DE-BABLED* DEFINITION of *all key* trilingual Nouns and Verbs in the verse under consideration.

Third, using the *Treasury of Scriptural Knowledge*, look up your few *very best* Parallel Passages and Proof Texts...*and de-Babel them*, the same way. *Now*, you've got the Gorilla Finger!

As my old Marine Corps Drill Instructor used to say, "That's aaallll they are to it!" Notice that we did not analyze anything but Nouns and Verbs—that's because about 95% of the time, that's all you need. The other 5% of the time? Just de-Babel some key modifiers. Almost everything is in the Nouns and Verbs, remember? If you have the primary meanings of the definitions and parsing of the Nouns and Verbs down pat, *you've got virtually everything the verse is saying.* If you face Contention, from a Doctor using Linguistic Quibble-lation, what's he going to do? He will try to use the other parts of speech to contrary you. How will that work? He can only do one of just two things: *Contrary* the proven primary meaning of key Nouns and Verbs, using the modifiers (then you simply point out where he is grammatically wrong—You win); or, *Support* the proven primary meaning of Nouns and Verbs with the modifiers (making your case even stronger—You win).

When you face Contention, from a Doctor using Linguistic Quibble-lation, just shove that gorilla finger right up his nose. Power in controversy is found in WHAT THE BIBLE *SAYS* AND *MEANS* IN PROOF TEXTS, not in doctoral doo-waddle using graduate level linguistic spoof and piffle.

(interregnum finis)

Lemme tell you a story about gorilla-fingering. Once upon a time, I was traveling out West, with a former Dean of the business school (Ph.D.) of a Prestigious Religious School in the South (whom I had converted and baptized). We were visiting a Pastor from that Prestigious Religious School (Ph.D), who was also on its board of directors. Together with him and the head of his deacon board, we visited a retired professor (Ph.D.) from Yale University Divinity School, who had preached and taught on all seven continents, and had also taught at that Prestigious Religious School in the South. We wound up discussing Regeneration BEFORE Faith (review pp. 83-88). He was arguing Faith BEFORE Regeneration, as a freewill condition for eternal salvation. As I taught you above, on p. 86, I cited him John 5:24, and pointed out that verse clearly stated Regeneration BEFORE Faith.

To the shock and surprise of everyone in the room, he literally *yelled* at me, "*Damnable heresy!*"

Taken aback, I carefully pointed out that *the Greek grammar, with parsing,* clearly placed Regeneration BEFORE Faith. I politely asked him, "If I have made a mistake in the Greek, please help correct my misunderstanding."

This time, he pounded on both chair arms with his fists, and shouted, "I *accept* the Greek, and I *deny* the Theology! *Damnable heresy!*" In other words: Yes it says that, but I don't believe it!

Can you say, "Gorilla finger?" *I knew you could!* By the way, if anybody tells you that Prestigious Religious School in the South was Bob Jones University, you didn't get that from me.

I repeat one more time. Power in controversy is found in WHAT THE BIBLE *SAYS* AND *MEANS* IN PROOF TEXTS, not in doctoral doo-waddle using graduate level linguistic spoof and piffle. I have shown you here, the way to achieve that power, and the confidence that goes with it. Not only does it glorify God and His Word...*it's FUN!*

ONE LAST THING

These tools make Bible study a lot more thorough, interesting, and precise. But, don't despair or delay getting started, if you don't have them. *Any* beat-up old Bible and ragtag piece of dictionary will do. The important thing above all is—**Read the Words of God in The Word of God!** Just remember to read carefully, to make sure what It *says*; and then check those word definitions carefully, to make sure what they *mean* (cp. Neh 8:8,12).

Bible Reading Tips

First, you have to have a *Plan of Attack*, some kind of strategy. Just opening the Bible and fumbling around for 20 or 30 minutes isn't productive. Here is an approach I have found very helpful. This simple *order* of books was taught me, years ago. I developed the *emphasis* on book groups myself. It stresses the New Testament over the Old Testament; and in the New Testament, Paul over the other writers. This is because you cannot understand the Old Testament without the New (2PE 1:19), and because Paul is the Apostle to us Gentiles, and has been set forth by Christ as a pattern for us (1TI 1:16).

READ PAUL FIRST

> Rom 11:13 For **I speak to you Gentiles, inasmuch as I am the apostle of the Gentiles**, I magnify mine office:
>
> 1Ti 1:16 Howbeit for this cause I obtained mercy, **that in me first Jesus Christ might shew forth** all longsuffering,

for **a pattern to them which should hereafter believe on him** to life everlasting.

Begin with the Book of Romans. This is basically Paul's overview of Christianity. Read through it *twice* before reading the rest of Paul.

Next, read Galatians, Ephesians, Philippians, and Colossians. There is a lot of doctrine in these little books. It has been observed that Ephesians overviews a lot of the material in Romans, and Galatians does likewise for Hebrews.

Then, read the rest of Paul, in any order you wish (I's and II's in order, of course). Pay close attention to the letters to the churches—we still have a lot of these problems to deal with.

Last, read the Book of Hebrews. This is Paul's explanation of the Old Testament system and the Jewish religion. Very helpful for Bible students to keep in mind.

READ PAUL TWICE, following this plan, *before* you read the rest of the New Testament. This will give you a thorough grounding in Paul's explanations of the Faith, and will greatly aid your understanding of the rest of the Bible. That is *why* he is The Apostle to the Gentiles.

READ THE REST OF THE NEW TESTAMENT (MINUS REVELATION)

First, read Luke and Acts. Luke was the traveling companion of Paul, and this gives you a Pauline view of the Life of Christ and the early history of the Church. Luke pictures Christ from the Gentile viewpoint and emphasizes Him as the Perfect Man.

Then, read John, which has been called the Church's gospel, and emphasizes the Deity of Christ.

Next, read the other Gospels. Note that Matthew is the Jewish gospel, and pictures Christ as the Promised King and Fulfillment of the Prophets (almost 25% is pointing out fulfilled prophecy). Mark has been called the Roman Gospel, and portrays Christ as the Perfect Servant.

Last, read the rest of the New Testament writers, *minus* the Book of Revelation. At this point, you will have a good grounding in the Faith of Christ. Leave Revelation until later. It was given by God 30+ years after the rest of the Bible was finished, is highly symbolical, *and must be read in light of the rest of the Bible.* Many people erroneously assume that Revelation is the key to The Bible. *Not so*—THE

Bible is the key to Revelation. So, become familiar with The Bible *before* you tackle Revelation, or you will be stumbling around in the dark—*I ga-ron-tee!*

READ THE NEW TESTAMENT TWICE

Read the New Testament again, *following the above pattern*: Read Romans twice, then read the rest of Paul; then, read Paul again the same way; then read the rest of the New Testament as recommended, minus Revelation.

At this point, you will have read through the New Testament twice, giving emphasis to the Apostle Paul (4x), and should have a *much* clearer understanding of the Christian Faith than ever before. Now, you are ready for the Old Testament.

Another mistake most people make is to assume that the Old Testament is the key to understanding the New Testament. *Not so*—THE NEW TESTAMENT IS THE KEY TO UNDERSTANDING THE OLD:

> 2Pe 1:19 **We have also a <u>more sure word</u> of prophecy; whereunto ye do well that ye take heed, as unto <u>a light that shineth in a dark place</u>**, until the day dawn, and the day star arise in your hearts:

Over 2/3 of the subject matter of the New Testament consists of explanations and applications of Old Testament teachings. *Only* with the clear light of the New Testament is a person prepared to wade through the types and shadows of the Old Testament. Trying to understand the Old Testament before one is thoroughly grounded in the New Testament is like trying to run a foot race blindfolded with your shoelaces tied together!

NOW, READ THE OLD TESTAMENT

Start with Genesis. It's not only the first book, but actually has been called the seedbed of the Scriptures, because almost all major doctrines have their beginnings in Genesis. Continue in order on through Malachi. The explanations of Old Testament events and types that you gained from a careful reading of the New Testament will *now* prove very meaningful to you. The *significance* of many things you've puzzled over in the past will now be obvious.

There are two books to pay special attention to: Psalms and Proverbs. Psalms contains some of the most comforting and instructive devotional writings in The Bible. Proverbs will give you more practical, everyday understanding of human nature and personality types than a Ph.D. in Psychology from any school. In fact, the opening verses of Proverbs tell us that the purpose of the book is:

Pro 1:2-4 To know wisdom and instruction; to perceive the words of understanding; To receive the instruction of wisdom, justice, and judgment, and equity; To give subtilty to the simple, to the young man knowledge and discretion.

Proverbs is an excellent book for daily meditations, in addition to regular Bible study. The book has 31 chapters—read one each day of the month (takes less than ten minutes), and you'll read it through 12 times in a year. No other source will give you a deeper or more useful understanding of human nature, for everyday life, than Proverbs.

NOW...DO IT ALL OVER AGAIN

Reread the New Testament twice, as instructed above; then read the Old Testament once more. At this point, you will have read Paul 8x, the rest of the New Testament 4x, and the Old Testament 2x.

Now, you are ready for Revelation.

AT LAST—READ REVELATION

Revelation is the most difficult and complicated book in the Bible. In fact, as I mentioned above, God did not even give us Revelations until some 30 years after the rest of the Bible (except possibly John's other writings) was finished. You must have a solid background in Bible history, prophecy, doctrine, and symbols before you can read much of Revelation profitably. The rest of the Bible is the key to Revelation, not the reverse. When trying to understand the symbols in Revelation, use a concordance to compare how each symbol was used elsewhere in Scripture. *Never* accept as the meaning of any symbol in Revelation an interpretation that cannot be shown for that symbol elsewhere in the Bible. For example, just try to find even one place in the Bible besides REV 6:2 where a white horse rider is the antichrist. There isn't one. How then can we know—absolutely *know* —from Bible usage what the white horse rider symbol represents? Use a concordance and look up all the occurrences of "white horse" in The Bible. There is *one* other, REV 19:11, and there it is clearly the Lord Jesus Christ, *not* the antichrist. In ZEC, we find white chariot horses, but that's not quite the same. Also, in REV 19:14, we find the armies in Heaven following Christ on white horses. Now you must choose between the majority of fundamentalist commentators, who tell you that the white horse rider of REV 6:2 is the antichrist, and your Bible's usage of the symbol, which shows the rider to be Christ. Big difference, huh? Some parts of Revelation are fairly clear and straightforward, but most of it is the most concentrated symbolism in the Bible. If you don't have a fair grasp of the rest of Scripture before trying to tackle it, you're going to get as confused as a termite in a yo-yo.

Read Revelation JUST ONCE—then, start reading The Bible all over again, as outlined above. This plan of Bible Reading will concentrate your knowledge where it needs to be—primarily on the writings of Paul, then on the rest of the New Testament. It will prepare you to understand the Old Testament much better than you otherwise would. Finally, it will give you the Bible background for understanding Revelation.

If you allow 30 minutes of daily Bible study, according to this plan, for 6 days a week, you will read through the Bible in 12-18 months, and will have a solid understanding of how the New Testament both fulfills and explains the Old. Save Sunday to study over the Sunday sermon, and other sermons you wish to review.

USE THE BOOK *A BRIEF REVIEW OF BIBLE DOCTRINE*

Many years ago, I wrote **A Brief Review of Bible Doctrine,** so the people I pastored would have a simple handbook, to review and brush up on basic Bible doctrines. It would be ideal, to flesh out the 7 Core Doctrines we have studied here. It is written in the form of a confession of faith, in the front section, with an extensive collection of mostly Proof Texts, with some notes, in the back section. It is based on the Confession John Gill wrote for his church, but includes information from a number of Baptist confessions, plus modern material the passage of over 250 years of history has made useful. All the basic stuff Christians should be very familiar today with is in there. It is also valuable for finding proof texts, to use in witnessing to others. It is my *intent*, God willing, to publish a slight update next year, and to make it available from the same sources as this book. We'll see.

Remember, always pray at the beginning and end of your study sessions, for God to open your mind and heart to receive and understand The Words of God in The Word of God:

> 2Co 4:6 For **God**, who commanded the light to shine out of darkness, **hath shined in our hearts, to give the light of the knowledge** of the glory of God in the face of Jesus Christ.
>
> Luk 24:45 Then **opened he** [Jesus] **their understanding**, that they might understand THE SCRIPTURES,
>
> Act 16:14 And a certain woman named **Lydia**, a seller of purple, of the city of Thyatira, which worshipped God, heard us: **whose heart the Lord opened, that she attended unto the things which were spoken of Paul.**

*****

Chapter 5—Some Final Thoughts

Now, Kind Reader, you know that The Bible is God's Inspired and Preserved Scripture. You know how to Study It and how to Read it. I have one last and supremely important piece of practical advice to give you:

Don't *EVER* forget it!

In over 50 years of being a Christian, I have seen individuals, churches, and denominations make a fatal and almost always irreversible mistake. It's probably the most frequent mistake folks make. They will be diddy-bopping along in their Christian life, thankful to God, Reading and Studying their Bibles and following all the concepts, Principles, and Rules of Bible Study; and then...*Wham!*...they run smack dab into a...SITUATION.

Whatever else it does, this SITUATION will put them clearly crosswise with The Bible. There will be something they want with all their heart; or something they conceive they positively must do; or some friend or family member, though in the wrong, it seems they absolutely must support.

Yet The Word of God says **NO**.

They will pour through concordances, commentaries, dictionaries, grammars and lexicons—yet The Word of God still says **NO**.

Then, they make **THE FATAL MISTAKE**. This SITUATION pulls so strongly upon their fleshly hearts that they just can't not do it. So, they...*CHANGE*...The Word of God (remember Mother Eve in the Garden?). Not a lot...just a *little* bit...just enough so that NO means YES. They *change* The Word of God to MEAN *the exact opposite of what It SAYS*. Besides, that SITUATION is so pleasant to the eyes, so needful to do, so plausibly the wisest move possible. *But it's the exact opposite of what The Word of God says.* So, they *change* The Word of God, or *ignore* The Word of God, or *deny* The Word of God...AND DO IT ANY DANG WAY. Oftentimes, they *then* become the most amazingly righteous Pharisees *about everything else;* just a-howlin' and a-slobberin', "Keep the holy Word-a-God, A-MAN!" But...they *do* what they dang well want to, in that SITUATION..."and The Word of God be damned," *so their actions say* (Matt 7:16-20). That is a foolish, a terrible, and almost always a fatal mistake.

> Isa 68:3b-4 ...<u>Yea, they have chosen their own ways</u>, and their soul delighteth in their abominations. 4 **I also will choose their delusions, and will bring their fears upon them**; because when I called, none did answer; when I

spake, they did not hear: but they did evil before mine eyes, and chose *that* in which I delighted not.

You see, Kind Reader, the Lord trieth the hearts of His Children (Psm 7:9) to bring us forth as gold (Job 23:10). But the disobedient and the wicked shall be destroyed (Psm 11:5). ***Never, ever, tinker with The Word of God.***

So, the single most important piece of practical advice about Bible Study that I offer you is: *Remember* Bible Study Rule #5—SUBMIT TO THE WORD OF GOD WHEN YOU UNDERSTAND IT.

DON'T *EVER* FORGET IT!

Ecc 12:13-14 Let us hear **THE CONCLUSION OF THE WHOLE MATTER**: Fear God, and keep his commandments: for this is the whole duty of man.
    14 For God shall bring every work into judgment, with every secret thing, whether it be good, or whether it be evil.

*****